THE
WAY
BACK
HOME

A Simple Guide to...

THE
WAY
BACK
HOME

JERRY SUTTON

BROADMAN
&HOLMAN
PUBLISHERS

Nashville, Tennessee

© 2002
by Jerry Sutton

0–8054–2497-0

Published by Broadman & Holman Publishers,
Nashville, Tennessee

Subject Heading: SPIRITUAL GROWTH

Unless otherwise noted, Scripture quotations are from the
NKJV, New King James Version, copyright © 1979, 1980,
1982, Thomas Nelson, Inc., Publishers.

1 2 3 4 5 6 7 8 9 10 06 05 04 03 02

DEDICATION

To all those at Rock Creek, Wedgwood, and Two Rivers
who found their way back home.

CONTENTS

PREFACE

I HAVE BEEN IN THE MINISTRY for over twenty years. In that time I have lost count of the number of times I have counseled believers who were away from the Lord and wanted to start over. Although I am aware of many great books for Christians, I am unaware of any that I could place in a Christian's hand and say, "Read this. It will tell you what to do. It will help you start over with God. It will help you find the way back home."

For all of you who have needed a game plan for getting back into fellowship with God, this volume is for you.

The Eight Steps

Step One   Be Honest with Yourself and God
Step Two   Confess to God
Step Three Disengage from the World
Step Four   Never Doubt God's Unconditional Love for You
Step Five   Give and Request Forgiveness
Step Six   Rejoice in Your Restored Fellowship
Step Seven Rebuild Broken Walls of Behavior and Belief
Step Eight Reconnect with and Reinforce Right
            Relationships

PARABLE OF THE PRODIGAL SON

Luke 15:11–32

THEN HE SAID: "A certain man had two sons. And the younger of them said to his father, 'Father, give me the portion of goods that falls to me.' So he divided to them his livelihood. And not many days after, the younger son gathered all together, journeyed to a far country, and there wasted his possessions with prodigal living. But when he had spent all, there arose a severe famine in that land, and he began to be in want. Then he went and joined himself to a citizen of that country, and he sent him into his fields to feed swine. And he would gladly have filled his stomach with the pods that the swine ate, and no one gave him anything. But when he came to himself, he said, 'How many of my father's hired servants have bread enough and to spare, and I perish with hunger! I will arise and go to my father, and will say to him, "Father, I have sinned against heaven and before you, and I am no longer worthy to be called your son. Make me like one of your hired servants."' And he arose and came to his father. But when he was still a great way off, his father saw him and had compassion, and ran and fell on his neck and kissed him. And the son said to him, 'Father, I have sinned against heaven and in your sight, and am no longer worthy to be called your son.' But the father said to his servants, 'Bring out the best robe and put it on him, and put a ring on his hand and sandals on his feet. And bring the fatted calf here and kill it, and let us eat and be merry; for this my son was dead and is alive again; he was lost and is found.' And they began to be merry. Now his older son was in the field. And as he came and drew near to the house, he heard music and dancing. So he called one of the servants and asked what these things meant. And he said to him, 'Your brother has come, and because he has received him safe and sound, your father has killed the fatted calf.' But he was angry and would not go in. Therefore his father came out and pleaded with him. So he answered and said to his father, 'Lo, these many years I have been serving you; I never transgressed your commandment at any time; and yet you never gave me a young goat, that I might make merry with my friends. But as soon as this son of yours came, who has devoured your livelihood with harlots, you killed the fatted calf for him.' And he said to him, 'Son, you are always with me, and all that I have is yours. It was right that we should make merry and be glad, for your brother was dead and is alive again, and was lost and is found.'"

INTRODUCTION

HER NAME WAS KAREN. She was young, smart, attractive, and absolutely miserable. Karen epitomized the truth that you cannot judge a book by its cover. I would never have guessed how unhappy she was. She told me her story about growing up in church and inviting Jesus into her heart as a child. Detailing her teenage years, she recounted the compromises she made in order to be accepted by her peers. And now, as a young adult she had habits that enslaved her, guilt that haunted her, and a constant uneasiness that "life was not supposed to turn out like this." "Can you help me?" she asked. To Karen, and those like her, this book is written.

So your life is a mess and you find yourself in a place you never intended to be. Or maybe it is not a mess, but you are not where you once were spiritually. And you are dissatisfied with your present status. Sad to say, that is the all-too-familiar story of many believers. The good news, however, is that your Heavenly Father desires for you to come back into fellowship with Him. The purpose of this book is to describe, step-by-step, how to get from where you are to where you want to be.

Jesus, the Master Communicator, told the story of the prodigal son. It is the story of a child who strayed and then returned to his father's home. But more than that, it is the story of hope. It is the story of a father's love that refused to concede his prodigal son was forever gone. It also could be Karen's story, or even yours.

Embedded in the words of this parable is a strategy for starting over with the God who loves to give a second chance. My assumption is that your relationship with God, once established, is secure, but that your fellowship with God depends on

1

your willingness to obey. I believe it is possible to lose your fellowship but not your relationship. I am convinced, moreover, that God is at work to restore that broken fellowship.

Because there is a tendency for the heart to stray, I offer this volume. For those who are tired of being out of fellowship and do not want to take the circuitous route home—like the wilderness route of the rebellious Israelites—this book offers a simple description of the shortest way back. Those who study geometry tell us that the shortest distance between two points is a straight line. This book will detail the "straight line" between where you are and where you want to be. May the Lord give you grace to start over.

PART I

JOURNEY TO THE FAR COUNTRY

RESTLESSNESS

For the great majority of mankind are satisfied with appearances,
as though they were realities and are often more influenced by the
things that seem than by those that are.
—Nicole Machiavelli

Satan, like a fisher, baits his hook according
to the appetite of the fish.
—Thomas Adams

Our corrupted hearts are the factories of the devil.
—Thomas Browne

"And the younger of them said to his father, 'Father, give me the
portion of goods that falls to me.'"
—Luke 15:12a

THE BIBLE IS FILLED with stories of believers and unbelievers
alike who sinned against God. For some it was a serious
breach of trust, for others a small almost inconspicuous com-
promise. In every case it began with a restless heart.

For the prodigal son, as he has come to be known, it began
with the belief that he was missing out on the good life. He
was driven by the desire to have more, experience more, see
more, do more. In that process he decided to disregard all
restraint, which included living in his father's house, under his
father's authority and watchful eye.

The prodigal son suffered from what I call the "grass is greener" syndrome, believing he was missing out. This subtle deception was first introduced in the Garden of Eden when Satan suggested to Eve that God was holding out on her.[1] From that time to now, one of Satan's primary assaults has been to tempt us with a subtle discontent or restlessness.

I have seen this restlessness take many forms. The teenage boy who feels he is missing out and concludes that a little experimentation with drugs will not hurt. The lonely wife addicted to the escape of an endless parade of soap operas. The weary traveler attracted to secret pornography in a hotel room. The young girl caught up in the rat race of popularity. The businessman who thinks that compromising his integrity to close the deal is a one-time exception. In each of these scenarios, the restless heart is enticed toward wanting what God forbids.

The prodigal son no doubt had heard of the far country— its parties, pleasures, and possibilities. With the lure of the far country his heart grew more and more restless. "I want what God forbids" is the subtle temptation every believer faces. For too many, I am afraid, the path of the prodigal becomes their reality. And so the song is played again and again.

Permit me to point out that a restless heart should be a sign to each of us that we need to run to our Heavenly Father for protection. Scripture teaches us that the Spirit of God who lives in us will identify the temptation for what it is.[2] Yet, too often we ignore the Spirit's warning or worse yet, we rationalize and mentally compartmentalize ourselves, altogether ignoring God's voice. To ignore a warning can be disastrous!

The worst industrial nuclear disaster in history occurred on April 26, 1986, in the town of Chernobyl in north central Ukraine of the former Soviet Union. It was caused by two electrical engineers who were playing around with one of the nuclear reactors. They were conducting an unauthorized experiment trying to see how long a turbine would freewheel (or keep spinning) when the power was turned off. To do this, they had to manually override six separate computer-driven alarm systems. Each time the computer would warn, *"Stop! Dangerous! Go no further!"* Each time the warning was foolishly disregarded. The end result was a major explosion, thirty-one immediate deaths, untold eventual deaths, and the release of 100 million curies of radionuclides into the atmosphere that circulated worldwide. Only time will determine the full extent and destruction of the accident.[3]

Often, we—like those foolish engineers—fail to heed the warning given to us by the Holy Spirit: *"Stop! Dangerous! Go no further!"* As a result, there comes a point when our restlessness and refusal to listen to the Spirit's warning leads us to cross the line from restlessness to rebellion.

How different human history might have been if Eve had cried out to God at the moment of temptation. Or, if only the prodigal had recognized the foolishness and potential misery bound up in his desire for freedom in the far country.

Years ago, my wife, Fern, and I were at the movies when the power surged and then cut off. In a few moments the power returned but when it did, it broke every tape in every projector in the entire theater. After twenty minutes and the assurance that ours would be fixed "any moment now," we debated whether to leave or stay. I suggested we take a look at the movie across the hallway, so we ducked into a five-minute clip of *Waterworld*.

The scene we saw had Kevin Costner, the hero, fighting a villain. After the enemy was defeated, all who rode on Costner's catamaran began to complain of intense hunger pain. In response to the complaints, he grabbed his trusty speargun and jumped off the boat, only to be pulled behind by a rope. It reminded me of trying to ski barefoot. The next thing you knew a great sea monster (a combination of a giant grouper and Jaws) moved in to eat Costner. Instead, he fired his speargun. And the monster, who thought Costner looked like lunch, turned out to be lunch.

What the sea monster did not understand was that Costner (the bait) had a hook (or in this case, a spear) in hand. The same is true with the enticement to sin. What glitters and stirs a restless hunger in us often has a hook we never anticipated. How tragic when we are caught by the lures of the world! By the way, is the devil dangling anything in front of you?

For the prodigal, his restlessness led to an unchallenged act of rebellion. It did not have to be that way. If only he had been like Daniel of old who "purposed in his heart not to defile himself. . . ." For each of us temptation is inevitable. How we respond to it is not. If only the prodigal had known and claimed the promise from Paul's pen: "No temptation has overtaken you except such as is common to man; but God is faithful, who will not allow you to be tempted beyond what you are able, but with the temptation will also make the way of escape, that you may be able to bear it."[4]

Yet your experience may be more akin to the prodigal's who, with the temptation, gave in. And your restless heart enticed you to walk away from fellowship with the Father and enter what we simply identify as "the far country."

2

REBELLION

To walk out of God's will is to step into nowhere.
—C. S. Lewis

Sin is blatant mutiny against God.
—Oswald Chambers

If sin was not such a pleasure it would not be such a problem.
—Author Unknown

"So he divided to them his livelihood. And not many days after, the younger son gathered all together, journeyed to a far country, and there wasted his possessions with prodigal living."
—Luke 15:12b–13

FOR THE PRODIGAL, what began with a restless heart proceeded to a rebellious act. A desire to live independent of God's will is the constant temptation for every believer.

As Jesus' parable unfolds, we discover the prodigal consolidating his resources and making a run for the border. Freedom's lure has blinded his vision of the tears in his father's eye. In his eagerness to indulge in the "world's delight," he is absolutely insensitive to his father's crushing pain.

When believers are enticed to sin, we tend to be desensitized to the pain we cause our Heavenly Father, not to mention the anguish we create for those who love us.

I am not saying that sin is not fun. Even the Bible points out that there is a pleasure in sin for a season.[1] The problem

9

with sin, however, is that it destroys. The prodigal, we are told, "journeyed to the far country, and there wasted his possessions with prodigal living." Permit me to elaborate.

The Far Country

The prodigal perceived the far country as a place of freedom. Restraints had been left behind and now he was on his own. The rules of the father's house no longer applied. I believe the "far country" is not so much a geographical location as it is a state of mind. It is the attitude that chooses to ignore God's standards in many or even just one area of our lives. It is the disposition that declares, "I am above God's laws." It is the assumption that "those laws just don't apply to me."

The sad commentary is that the rules the prodigal thought were restrictions were in fact given by his father as protection. And moving to the far country meant now he was fair game for Satan's attacks.

It is my experience that if we have a weakness, Satan will exploit it to our demise. Whether he is neutralizing our witness or placing us in great bondage, his ultimate goal is to destroy the work of God. And for many believers, the little sins that start out as unswept cobwebs in the recesses of our hearts soon become massive chains that hold us in hideous bondage.

Wasted His Possessions

We are all on the meter. By this I mean that our lives are measured in small units of time. And time marches on. When we choose to live in the far country we waste our most precious irreplaceable resource—our very lives. "Dost thou love life?" Ben Franklin asked. "Then do not squander time; for that's the stuff life is made of."[2]

The prodigal wasted more than his possessions. By increments, he was throwing away his life. I only wish he had heeded the prayerful words of Moses, "So teach us to number our days, that we may gain a heart of wisdom."[3] In simple language Moses was saying that when we fail to see the brevity of life we tend to live foolishly. Such was the case of the prodigal son.

Prodigal Living

The prodigal found himself on the fast track of life. There was no pleasure that he did not pursue. He emerged as a man of the world. The King James Version uses the phrase "riotous living." His was the unrestrained lifestyle of the rich and famous, or maybe the term should be *infamous*. The latest Hollywood film star and the reigning athletic superhero had nothing on this old boy. He had arrived! Or so he thought. *If my friends could only see me now* was probably echoing through the recesses of his mind.

Yet deeper in this prodigal's heart remained a gnawing emptiness. And what little remained of his mostly seared conscience continued to scream, *This is not who you are,* in those unguarded moments. *Yet who has time to worry about those sorts of things,* he rationalized. For him it was party time!

The danger with an indulgent lifestyle is that eventually a person can only stand so much pleasure and he or she begins to hit a place of burnout. Crash and burn is descriptive of more than just airplanes and cars.

In my teenage years one of the best friends I had was a fellow named Travis. He was as cool as anyone around. Yet Travis lived with a constant fear that "mom would do it again." In failing to handle appropriately a great disappointment in life, she turned to the escape of a combination of prescription drugs and alcohol. She was the first addict I ever knew. This was her far country.

Although there were times when she did very well, we never knew when she would go off the deep end again. I can remember to this day the awful pain in Travis's eyes when we would have to pick up his mom from where she was being held for public drunkenness. One day she took too many pills and drank too much vodka, and the great escape of these pleasures led to a premature death and children with permanent emotional scars.

Many pleasures in our society carry terminal price tags. I think of a young man I know. In the loneliness of a broken relationship, he indulged in what I call that "no one will ever know" behavior. And now when he should be experiencing the thirty-something excitement of upward social mobility, he faces the regimen of AZT and a battery of other medicines that have assisted in prolonging his AIDS-ravaged body.

I could tell you of many others who believed they were the exception to the rule. But you could probably make your own list. Worse yet, the person staring back at you in the mirror may be the very one who must admit, "I never intended to be like this."

Perhaps you heard the story of the old farmer and his wife. They were driving down the road one day, and the wife began to reminisce about how they used to sit close, how he used to put his arm around her, and how they cuddled when they drove in the old pickup truck. But now she seemed always to sit as close to the door as possible. Waiting for a moment before giving his response, the old farmer finally said, "I never moved."

So it is with God. When we run away from fellowship with Him and pursue a prodigal lifestyle, it is not God who moved. We moved. Like the prodigal we have hitched the wagon of our lives to the illusive delights of the far country and we find ourselves in a place we never intended. Yet remember, God never moved.

When Jesus said, "I will never leave you nor forsake you,"[4] He gave no qualifications or contingencies. His is not a performance-based acceptance. He still loves us. Yet He does not approve of the path the prodigals have taken. The old maxim "love the sinner, hate the sin" still applies.

If you are finding yourself in the far country, I want to encourage you to read on. There is hope for you.

3

REVERSAL

Out of the frying pan, into the fire.
—Tertullian

God wants our attention and He knows how to get it.
—James Earl Massey

*The Lord has a golden sceptre and an iron rod. Those who will
not bow to the one, shall be broken by the other.*
—Thomas Watson

Better shun the bait than struggle in the snare.
—John Dryden

*"But when he had spent all, there arose a severe famine in that
land, and he began to be in want. Then he went and joined himself
to a citizen of that country, and he sent him into his fields to feed
swine. And he would gladly have filled his stomach with the pods
that the swine ate, and no one gave him anything."*
Luke 15:14–16

THE POT OF GOLD at the end of his rainbow finally ran dry for
the prodigal son. And it began to rain, not just cats and dogs,
more like lions and tigers. He made a quick transition from
party to pity. Now he was experiencing the anguishing reality
in which his sin finally caught up with him. Remember the
hook?

Part of his problem was his own sinful irresponsibility. Coupled with that was a famine that encompassed the land. As a result, the Scripture says succinctly, "he began to be in want." You might say that Jesus was a master at understatement. The prodigal had no one to turn to. There were no Western Unions through which to send relief. His friends lasted as long as the money. Now both were gone.

One thing Jesus is communicating here is that God knows how to get our attention. When we as His children stray from Him, He will do whatever is necessary to bring us back into fellowship with Himself. When a Christian sins, the Holy Spirit immediately brings conviction. *"Stop! Dangerous! Go no further!"* Yet if we refuse to heed, He will take increasingly severe measures to get our attention.

Severe Measures

I have discovered that God has a variety of ways to get our attention. When the Israelites were wandering in the wilderness, they complained about not having meat—only manna. Finally Scripture says, "And He gave them their request, but sent leanness into their soul."[1] There are times when God, in His permissive will, allows us to stray. Yet the result will be that we will dry up spiritually. By this, I am not saying we shall be saved and lost again; rather, we will be miserable. And when the circumstances change, we will find ourselves in a wretched condition.

There are times when God will take our health. Did Paul not say in the context of the Lord's Supper, referring to believers who refused to live righteously, that "many are weak and sickly among you?" Paul's point is that sometimes God's chastening of our lives takes the form of physical illness. I do not believe all sickness is a result of sin, but some of it obviously is.

At other times God chastens us, or gets our attention, by threatening our financial security or even drying up the finances. This certainly was the case for the prodigal son. His riches-to-rags transition comes rather abruptly.

I have a friend, Gary, who is one of the finest salesmen I have ever known. He has done incredibly well. Yet, by his own admission he has related to me that there have been times in his life when his heart has strayed from faithful devotion to the Lord. And invariably those are the times when God has restricted the income. When finances get tight, we need to ask, "Lord, are you speaking to me?"

The Bible relates the story of a man named Achan, who during the time of the Israelite conquest of Canaan, took some things that did not belong to him. He thought no one would ever find out. Yet, his disobedience precipitated the Israelites' first loss, creating massive problems. Joshua, who at that period of history served as the leader of the Jewish nation, began to cry out to God, "Why have you let us down?" God's response was abrupt, "There is sin in the camp!" The Bible teaches that the defeat of an enterprise can be a result of hidden sin. How is it with you? Are there any hidden sins? Let me remind you of the prophet's message of old, "Beware, your sin will find you out!"[2]

King David believed his bases were all secure. Having committed adultery with Bathsheba, he covered his sin by arranging to have her husband killed in battle. So he sinned, he covered it with more sin, then pretended it never happened. Modern man has nothing on him! He forgot one thing, however. No sin is hidden to the watching eyes of Almighty God. This is an important lesson for each of us to remember.

In His wisdom the Lord sent a prophet, Nathan, to confront David with his sin. To his credit we can report that David turned from his sin in brokenness when it was finally exposed. His prayer of repentance is recorded for us in the fifty-first Psalm. Sometimes God sends someone to confront us with our sin.[3]

Then again, I have seen God get someone's attention by blessing them and prospering them. Although, to me, I have thought, *This does not seem fair*, I am reminded of Paul's statement, "Do you not know that the goodness of God leads you to repentance?"[4]

In all these ways, and I am sure more besides, God gracefully gets our attention. He has no desire to leave us in the far country even if it requires sending a major reversal into our lives.

One of the most colorful figures in Scripture was a man named Samson. When first introduced, we are told that "the child grew, and the Lord blessed him." Samson, as you might recall, was blessed with incredible strength, which he used to resist the occupying armies of the Philistines. Yet, Samson had a weakness for women and especially for a woman named Delilah. In fact, because of her seductive charm, he revealed to her that his source of strength was in his hair. "Cut my hair and I will be like other men," he admitted. Because of Samson's restless heart, which led to a rebellious heart and a riotous lifestyle, his place of leadership was squandered.[5]

Delilah passed along the secret of Samson's strength, his hair was cut, he was seized, and his eyes were pierced out. Then he was bound with leg irons and "ground grain in the prison house." Like an ox, he found himself walking in circles, a grinder of grain turning a millstone.[6]

Samson, whose calling in life was to be a great leader, found his life virtually ruined because he could not control his passions. His rebellious heart led to disaster. And it took this tragedy for his heart to turn back to the Lord. The final episode of Samson's life finds him with restored strength and one more opportunity to resist the Philistines. In his blindness, he was chained between two load-bearing pillars in the temple of Dagon, the Philistine god. Calling out to the Lord, Samson pled again for his strength. He then pulled down the pillars, destroying the temple and all who were in it.

Samson's life and death are a constant reminder for me to guard my heart. God used the brutality of an avenging army to get Samson's attention. Yet, though his heart did turn back to the Lord, be mindful of the opportunity he missed.[7]

Two Important Questions

What happens, you ask, to a believer who refuses the disciplining hand of God? Paul tells us that "many sleep," which is Paul's way of relating the truth that some believers die before they should. The Book of Acts records for us an incident of two believers, a husband and wife, who sinned against God. The end result was that they died young. Any time a believer sins against the Lord, chooses to live independently of God, and refuses to turn back to the Lord, I believe that person is a candidate for an untimely death. Are all early deaths a result of rebellion? I do not believe so. Yet, I have known people who, I am convinced, died before they should have because they refused to listen to God's voice.[8]

I learned this lesson in a very painful way. Our family pet, Abner, was a five-year-old golden retriever. He would play fetch for an hour at a time. I would throw the ball, and he would retrieve it over and over. I really loved that dog.

I must admit that there were times when the Lord taught me through my relationship with Abner. And the main lesson I learned was unconditional love. No matter what was going on in my life (I could be having a great day or a rough day; I could be optimistic or depressed), no matter what, I could walk out on my deck, and Abner would stop what he was doing and give me all kinds of unconditional love. He was always glad to see me even if I woke him up from a nap or went out in the middle of the night. He was a great dog.

Yet Abner had a character flaw. If he could get out of the yard, he would run! Now, he lived in a semi-spacious fenced-in backyard with lots of squirrels to chase. There was a big deck to sleep under and two dog houses, which he virtually ignored. In fact, we built the fence so he would have a place to call his own. As with the rest of the family, we wanted him to have a secure home.

When Abner was five years old, we moved from one house to another. To accommodate him, I had a fence built around the backyard of our new home. What I did not realize was that between the steps leading up to the deck and the rail, there was just enough room for a curious and character-flawed golden retriever who liked to get out and run to escape. I am sure that in his five-year-old golden retriever mind, that looked like an opportunity too good to pass up. In fact, he probably perceived the fence as somewhat restrictive of his personal desire to explore his world. What I placed for his protection, he perceived as my attempt to restrict his freedom and fun.

The truth is, we sometimes see God's restrictions the same way. He sets fences in our lives, not to keep us from having a fulfilling life, but to protect us. And too often we get busy seeing how we can escape those restrictions. What God intends for good, we see as His attempt to keep us from having fun. It is almost as though we are blind to the dangers and perils of sin.

It was a Sunday afternoon. My family was walking out the back door to the garage on our way to evening services at church. And there we found Abner laying down in the garage. I walked up to him and petted his head. He was not moving. In fact, his front legs were already a little stiff. I nudged him on the side like I had done hundreds of times and, still, no movement. I tried to open one of his eyes. Nothing. While we had been inside that afternoon, Abner had made his great escape to freedom. What he did not know was that our new neighborhood had lots of cars, many of which exceeded the speed limit. Evidently he had gotten into the street and been hit. I wish the person who hit him would have stopped, but that is another story. He had crawled back into the yard and into the garage and died of massive injuries. What he saw as an opportunity for fun proved to be his undoing. And there are times, I am sure, that what we perceive as an opportunity for pleasure also has a deadly payoff. If only Abner would have stayed within his boundaries, he would be with us today. The same can be said, I am sure, of some straying Christians.

A second important question is this: How do you understand it when a person claims to be a Christian, sins repetitively, and seems to have no chastening by God? God tells us,

"If you are without chastening, of which all [His children] have become partakers, then you are illegitimate and not sons."[9] The bottom line is this. If you claim to be a Christian and continue to sin and God does nothing to discipline you, the truth is you are simply a label without content. You are not an authentic believer.

This grave fact should cause each of us to heed the declaration of Paul to "examine yourselves as to whether you are in the faith."[10]

A Sobering Reminder

Let me offer a sobering reminder to you. One of the great principles of Scripture is identified simply as the "Law of the Harvest." Paul put it this way, "Do not be deceived, God is not mocked; for whatever a man sows, that he will also reap."[11] When it comes to our attitudes, actions, and ambitions, we reap what we sow, more than we sow, later than we sow, and sometimes even others will reap what we sow. There is no escaping the Law of the Harvest. If for no other reason than this, each of us should daily pursue an ongoing, intimate, personal relationship with Jesus Christ.

For our prodigal friend, the end of his downward journey was a pagan pigpen. Minimally this was humiliating to a young Jewish man who grew up with a kosher lifestyle. Coupled with the humiliation was an incredible hunger. God finally had his attention. The issue is, does He have yours? What is God saying to you right now? What next?

4

REGRET

I have to live with myself, and so
I want to be fit for myself to know,
I want to be able as days go by
Always to look myself in the eye;
I don't want to stand, with the setting sun,
And hate myself for the things I've done.

—Edgar Guest

For who, alas, has lived,
Nor in the watches of the night recalled
Words he has wished unsaid and deeds undone?

—Samuel Rogers

"But when he came to himself, he said, 'How many of my father's
hired servants have bread enough and to spare, and I perish
with hunger!'"

—Luke 15:17

JESUS MADE AN INTERESTING STATEMENT when he told us that the prodigal son, "came to himself," or as another translation says he "came to his senses." Our prodigal friend finally woke up and smelled the coffee, or in his case the stench. What full-bodied aroma!

It is a wonderful day when we finally come to the place where we see things correctly. The Bible calls this "wisdom." It is the ability to see life from God's perspective. How do you get wisdom? The Bible tells us that if we lack it, we can ask

God for it, and He will give it to us. One stipulation comes with this promise. When we receive it, we must act on it. If we refuse to act on the wisdom God gives to us—that is, with faith or trusting obedience—God tells us that we are wasting our time.

If you find yourself captive to a sinful habit and realize you are far away from God, ask the Lord to help you return to Him. I often ask our church family, "Have you ever been closer to God than you are right now?" I ask myself the same question. Then I remind our folks, like the old farmer's retort, God did not move.

Now just because the prodigal understood where he was—"he came to himself"—did not mean he was delivered. In fact, he was still in the mud with the pigs. He was still malnourished and was even tempted to eat the food he was feeding the pigs. In other words, he was still in bad shape. Yet the first step on the journey back is found right here.

I want to share with you eight steps that constitute the shortest way back to fellowship with God. This is a simple biblical pattern.

Step One—Be Honest with Yourself and God

The first step to getting back into fellowship with the Lord is simply to be honest with yourself and God. It is taking responsibility for your choices and actions. It is saying, "I blew it."

We live in an "it's not my fault, I'm a victim" society where people have been taught not to take responsibility for their actions. As long as we take that posture, we will never be in fellowship with God. In fact, I am convinced that one of Satan's biggest lies is to convince people they are victims and therefore not responsible.

God teaches us clearly that we are responsible! We are responsible for our own actions and also our reactions. We are responsible for the choices we make, the way we invest our time, resources, and influence. Moreover, we are responsible for the right things we failed to do. If this is so, then to accept it as such is a big step in the right direction.

Let me warn you about a trap many people face—the "blaming" trap. There are times when we are hurt, or we give in to sin, and we want to blame someone for our actions or reactions. I believe there are times when that is the first step away from fellowship with God. It may have been that the prodigal pointed to his father and said, "He is so unfair to me. I want out." Or perhaps he blamed his older brother, "He's always picking on me," or "Dad loves him best."

Perhaps the prodigal thought home was too oppressive and blamed the strictness of home for his choice to leave. That easily could have been the case. Yet, in spite of the circumstances at home, the truth is he chose to leave. No one made that decision for him. And to blame anyone else for his own choice was really another exercise in futility.

In Texas, where I used to live, they call that a dry well. You can dig there all you want, but you are just wasting time.

One of my best friends in the world, Brad Rudge, is a medical doctor. Periodically he has seen patients become terminally ill because in the early stage of an illness, they were in denial. They pretended nothing was wrong. They ignored the symptoms until it was too late to do anything about them. What happens physically can also happen spiritually.

Please, be honest with yourself and God about where you are spiritually. I assure you that Jesus, who is also called "the Great Physician," is ready to help you understand where you are and help you return to where you need to be.

Understanding Where You Are

Once you have made the decision to get honest and be responsible for your actions, you need to gain an understanding of where you are. An accurate assessment is the order of the day. The prodigal put it this way, "I perish with hunger." You cannot get much plainer than that.

The issue for you is this: How can you gain that accurate assessment and understanding of where you are spiritually?

Let me suggest a method. Block some time to think, reflect, and pray. In that time keep a notebook and pen handy so you can write down what you see. If you prefer a laptop, use that. Begin to pray, asking the Lord to show you what is wrong. As the Lord shows you things, write them down. The issue for you is to discover God's assessment. If you ask, you will receive.[2]

I base this on two principles. First, God desires us to be in right relationship and true fellowship with Him more than we want to experience it. I take Jesus at His word when He said, "Come to Me, all you who labor and are heavy laden [under a heavy weight], and I will give you rest."[3] The worst weight I know is the weight of guilt and sin. I am convinced that many psychiatric institutions would empty overnight if patients only learned the secret of getting free from the burden of guilt and sin.

The second principle comes again from the lips of Jesus. He promised that when He returned to heaven He would send His Spirit into this world. The Holy Spirit would have at least three responsibilities applicable here. He would convince (or convict) the world of the reality of three things: sin in our lives, God's standard of righteousness, and the awesome fact of the coming judgment. It is the Holy Spirit's job to show us our sin.[4]

Permit me to point out a distinction that might easily be a stumbling block if you are not careful. When the Holy Spirit brings conviction, He is very specific in pointing out our sin. In fact, I am convinced that He deals only in specifics. The counterfeit to Holy Spirit conviction is satanic condemnation. I describe it as a feeling of badness or a general sense of failure. The devil's condemnation is always general and leads to darkness and oppression. If the uneasy feeling is not specific, I write it off as condemnation. Paul said, "There is therefore now no condemnation to those who are in Christ Jesus."[5]

The Spirit's conviction is specific, provides light, and leads to liberty. Jesus promised, "If the Son makes you free, you will be free indeed." Paul added, "And where the Spirit of the

Lord is there is liberty."⁶ The greatest freedom I know is the
freedom of a clean conscience. And it begins with an honest
and accurate assessment of where you are. Ask the Lord and
He will show you. The issue for you is this—will you stop
long enough to listen to God?

I learned this principle from a retired missionary to China,
Miss Bertha Smith. In her late seventies when she instructed
me, at an age when most people are ready to slow down and
take it easy, she was going full speed ahead, helping folks like
me learn the reality of freedom in Christ. Thank you, Miss
Bertha!

Understanding Where You Could Be and Should Be

At long last, our prodigal remembers who he is—"How
many of my father's hired servants have bread enough and to
spare." The definitive words here are not food-related but
family-related—"my father."

In all of the prodigal's wanderings he has never ceased to
be his father's son. Many words can describe him.
Backslidden. Sinful. Rebellious. Our list could go on and on.
Yet the fact remains—he is his father's son. And that central
truth overrides every other consideration.

The same is true for you. No matter what you have done
or failed to do, you are a child of God if you can look back
to a point in time when you surrendered your life to Jesus
Christ. When that occurred you were birthed into God's family. The Bible calls that being saved. Unfortunately, we who
are God's children do not always act like it. Nonetheless,
God's desire for you is that you not only have a right relationship secured for you by Jesus' sacrificial death on the
cross, but also that you experience an ongoing fellowship
with Him day by day.

In our story it is the difference between living in the
father's house and existing in the far country. God never
intended for you to be out of fellowship with Him. He hates
it when you choose to live in the far country.

Many times I have seen people get depressed because of the distance between where they are and where they should be. In fact, when people lose hope that they can bridge the gap, believing it is impossible, the resulting emotion is depression. No matter what you have done or failed to do, if you are willing to return to your Heavenly Father, He is more than willing to receive you and restore you to fellowship with Himself.

When I was a teenager, space travel was getting pretty routine. In fact, it was so commonplace that the network news considered launches a nonevent and did not even cover them. Walking on the moon was now "old hat." Then something happened to change all that. *Apollo 13*, which started out as one more ho-hum round-trip, experienced an onboard explosion in space, and suddenly the world's attention focused on whether or not our astronauts would make it home. Numerous obstacles were present—low fuel, low electricity, insufficient communication, and inexperience, to name a few.

As the space module was preparing for reentry into earth's atmosphere, several new problems emerged with respect to trajectory and velocity. If they came in too steep the module would burn up because of the atmosphere. On the other hand, if their approach was too flat, it was possible for the astronauts to skip off the atmosphere into space like a rock skipping on water. The most unnerving part was that they only had one opportunity to get back; there would be no second chance.

Too often, we think of getting back into fellowship with God the same way—too many obstacles, compounded by a fear of failure, and an attitude that says "What's the use?" The voice of the devil, coupled with our own insecurity, tells us it is mission impossible.

At this point we need to be reminded that God, who is all-powerful and all-knowing, is more desirous than we are for us to return to fellowship with Him. And He is able to bring us back if we are willing to return, even with obstacles that seem impossible to overcome. God is able. He gives second chances. Even more, He stands ready for us to come home.

Now, in light of that, how do you get back to where you once belonged?

PART II

RETURN FROM THE FAR COUNTRY

5

REPENTANCE

Repentance must be something more than mere remorse for sins: it comprehends a change of nature befitting heaven.
—Lew Wallace

Let the quantity of thy sins be the measure of thy repentance.
——Isaac Bargrave

You cannot repent too soon, because you do not know how soon it will be too late.
—Thomas Fuller

'I will arise and go to my father, and will say to him, "Father, I have sinned against heaven and before you, and I am no longer worthy to be called your son. Make me like one of your hired servants."'
—Luke 15:18–19

NOTICE WHAT IS HAPPENING to our prodigal friend. His whole attitude has changed from "give me" to "make me," from self-will to submission. The biblical word for this change is *repentance*. Before he journeyed back to his father's house, he cried out to God in confession and repentance—"I have sinned against heaven." I see in this his confession to God. As we examine this concept more closely, let me tell you a story that sheds light on what I am saying. As a boy growing up in Mobile, Alabama, I had certain chores for which I was responsible. One of these was cutting the grass, a chore I alternated with my twin brother. I would cut one week and he would cut the next. Because of the rainfall it was almost a weekly task.

One evening dad told me the grass needed cutting the next day. "Yes, sir!" The next day came and I got busy playing ball, watching television, and other things kids like to do in the summer time. In fact, I absolutely forgot about cutting the grass . . . until supper.

When I saw my dad I remembered. I actually was hoping he forgot, although I knew better. I did not look at him or talk to him. I was a guilt-ridden thirteen-year-old. I could hardly swallow because of the lump in my throat. All I could think of was how much trouble I was in. When supper was over and I thought there might be a glimmer of hope, Dad spoke up. "Jerry, is there something you forgot today?" I was ready to crawl under the table. Finally, I broke my silence and through my tears told him I was sorry and asked for forgiveness, which I quickly received. I then went out and did what I should have done earlier.

No matter what I did, or in this case failed to do, I remained my father's son. It was a matter of birth and blood. It was impossible for me to cease being part of the family. On the other hand, by my irresponsibility, which was a form of disobedience, I broke the fellowship with my dad. In fact, I almost dreaded seeing him. And I felt that way until the issue was resolved by my confession and repentance.

The same principle holds true with our relationship to our Heavenly Father. I will always be His child because of my salvation brought about by being "born again" into His family. Yet, by my sinful choices—which may be wrong ambitions, attitudes, or things I did or failed to do—I break my fellowship with my Heavenly Father. Such was the case of the prodigal son—sonship intact, fellowship in shambles!

The issue for us is, how do you restore the fellowship?

Step Two—Confess to God

In a short letter written by John the Apostle, I discovered a very liberating truth. "If we confess our sins, He [God] is faithful and just to forgive us our sins and to cleanse us from all unrighteousness." I believe this verse is the key to restoring fellowship with our Heavenly Father. The wisest man who ever lived, King Solomon, wrote essentially the same thing, warning, "He who covers his sins will not prosper, but whoever confesses and forsakes them will have mercy."[1]

When it comes to sins, we can deal with them one of two ways. We can cover them, which means deal with them our way. Or we can confess and forsake, which is dealing with them God's way. People cover sins by rationalizing them, calling them a habit, by compartmentalizing their minds and ignoring that compartment, by excusing them, by blaming someone else for them or even by procrastinating—"I will deal with them . . . tomorrow." Those ways of dealing with sins simply prolong the estrangement. By the way, have you been covering anything?

God's way of dealing with sins is to confess them, which Solomon explained entailed both confessing and forsaking them. It means to admit them and quit them.

The word *confess* means literally to "say the same thing." It is agreeing with God's assessment that those things are wrong and must be forsaken. I believe it can include the emotion of regret, although the critical component is the choice to turn away from and cease indulging in the sin.

Some schools of thought teach that because all of our sins—past, present, and future—have been dealt with at the cross, and because we have received God's free grace gift of salvation, then we need only acknowledge that sin is sin. We do not need to confess each sin as the Spirit brings it to our remembrance. In other words, the confession about which I write is no longer necessary.

I believe *that* idea has been caused by a combination of three things. First, a misreading of the teachings of Scripture. Second, an overcompensation toward those who have been hurt spiritually because of their never-ending ride on Satan's guilt trip, a spiritual treadmill if you please. And third, it is also a reaction toward those who see in my understanding a works orientation. For the most part I also believe this mind-set has damaged the Kingdom of God by communicating that some sinfulness is to be expected. At its root is the failure to distinguish between relationship and fellowship, and accept-ance and approval.

It also stops short of distinguishing between sin issues and maturity issues. By this I mean that sometimes people confuse immaturity with disobedience. Several years ago, I walked into the house at supper time and told Ashli, my oldest daughter, that tomorrow I wanted her to cut the yard while I was at work. When I arrived home—this is a generational thing—the yard was not even touched. When I came in, I asked her why she did not do what I said. Her response? "Dad, I'm only five years old." My point is this. She could not have cut the yard even if she wanted to. You see, this did not revolve around issues of rebellion, defiance, or disobedience. It was a maturity issue. Yet, for today's prodigals the issues are not maturity-related but sin issues that must be addressed.

So here you are. You know your relationship is secure but your fellowship is damaged. Where do you go from here? I want to urge you to take Scripture literally where you are told to "confess your sins." If you will do that, God, because He is faithful and righteous, will do two things. First, He will for-give you for those things—sins—which have broken your fel-lowship with Him. Also, He will cleanse you from them. In other words, He will change us, even take away the desire to do those things about which we are now ashamed.

Earlier, you wrote out your list of sins as the Lord showed you. These included ambitions, attitudes, activities, things you said, and likely other things that you have omitted doing. The Holy Spirit pointed out these things as wrong and you owned up to them by writing them down. Now, take your list, which should be confidential, and go through each item. "Lord, I confess that I cheated on that math test." "I confess

I lied to my partner." "I confess I have not given You your tithe."

Go through your entire list. Confess each one to the Lord. Tell Him you choose to forsake your sin and claim His forgiveness and cleansing. Remember that forgiving and cleansing are God's responsibilities, not yours. We confess, and He forgives and cleanses. We do our part. He does His. Now cross the items off of your list. It has been dealt with God's way. Remember, what God forgives, He forgets!

For most people, this time of reflection, prayer, and confession under the guidance of God's Holy Spirit is a major spiritual milestone. A word of caution is in order. If the sin you identify is not specific, it is not something the Holy Spirit is addressing. He deals in specifics. Also, once you have confessed a sin, take God at His word that it is forgiven and cleansed. Our emotions can be deceptive at this point.

Some time ago a man named David came to see me. He was consumed with guilt and remorse over an adulterous affair that had occurred years before. I asked him why he had not confessed it to the Lord and received His forgiveness and cleansing. His response was that he had asked the Lord to forgive him a thousand times. My counsel to David was that he should have confessed it once and then thanked God 999 times for His forgiveness and cleansing. Many times we remain in bondage because we do not in simple childlike faith take God at His Word when He said if we will confess, He will cleanse and forgive.

Now, let me warn you of a trap the devil loves to spring on people. We are tempted, we give in, and we begin to feel guilty. Maybe it is a sin we have committed before. Perhaps it is so hideous that we begin to believe the devil's lies, "You can't take that to God again." "You told him last time you'd never do it again." "God won't forgive you for that—again." "That one is too bad—don't go back to God until you've straightened up your life." These are lies from the devil.

I heard the story some time ago of a businessman whose shirts were dirty and needed to go to the cleaners. He threw the shirts into the trunk of his car and promptly forgot about them. He also forgot when he changed a flat tire the week before that he had left the jack laying loose in the trunk. Several days passed and the man remembered his shirts and took them to the cleaners.

When he opened the trunk to get the shirts out, they not only had the normal dirtiness but were also streaked by the grease from the jack. They were a mess! When the business-man walked into the cleaners with his dirty shirts, he began to apologize for bringing in such filthy clothes. The young lady at the desk broke in abruptly and said, "Don't apolo-gize—that's why we're here! If you could take care of them yourself you wouldn't need us."

Dear friend, God feels the same way as that young lady at the cleaners: "Don't apologize. That's why I am here. If you could clean yourself up, you would not need Me." We come to God, just as we are and He takes it from there! We come. We confess. He cleanses. He forgives. That is God's way for us to deal with our sins.

Remember that ultimately all sin is against God.[2] It is His forgiveness and cleansing we need. If a sin is big enough to remember, it is serious enough to confess to God. He does not want us to cover our sins but confess and forsake them. Will you do that?

Once you are up-to-date with God, I encourage you to cul-tivate the habit of keeping a short account with Him. When the Spirit convicts you of a sin, confess it immediately. Guard your fellowship with God. Remember that confession is the key that unlocks the door to fellowship with God. For our prodigal friend it is the final step before the journey home.

6

Return

When you follow Christ it must be a total burning of all your
bridges behind you.

—Billy Graham

And while the lamp holds out to burn, the vilest
sinner may return.

—Isaac Watts

"And he arose and came to his father. But when he was still a
great way off, his father saw him and had compassion, and ran
and fell on his neck and kissed him."

—Luke 15:20

OUR PRODIGAL FRIEND now begins his journey home. Jesus
said simply, "He arose and came to his father." No one knows
how far he had to travel or what obstacles were in his way.
We do know that his sights were on home and particularly on
reconnecting with his father.

We need to be very clear on one thing. He chose to leave
and now he is choosing to return. As in the story of the prodigal son, I believe most people experience as much of God as
they want. Let's follow our prodigal as he begins the journey
home.

Step Three—Disengage from the World

Finally, the prodigal makes his move. Up to this point he
has thought about leaving, dreamed of home, and probably

had been through a series of self-condemnations. He has confessed his sins to God, but now comes that incredible moment. What he has thought about he finally does. He takes to heart the admonition, "Just do it!" And he does. He begins his long journey home.

One of the most difficult parts of getting back into fellowship with God is disengaging from the world. The concept *world* has multiple uses in Scripture and I certainly want to be clear. It says "God so loved the world." This refers, by context, to the people in the world. "Red and yellow, black and white, they are precious in His sight, Jesus loves the little children of the world," is certainly true. This is not the "world" from which we are to disengage.[1]

In the same letter cited earlier, the apostle John went on to say, "Do not love the world or the things in the world. If anyone loves the world, the love of the Father is not in him." A contradiction? Hardly. At this point we are being warned against following after the world system, which refuses to acknowledge God's rightful place. The apostle continued, "For all that is in the world—the lust of the flesh, the lust of the eyes, and the pride of life—is not of the Father but is of the world."[2]

These things refer to that which drew the prodigal to the far country in the first place. They include the desire to gratify our lusts, the pursuit of having what is not ours, and taking a posture of self-sufficiency. Certainly our prodigal found himself among this crowd. Yet, sad to say, when he finally got what he wanted, he did not want what he got. Ultimately, the world does not satisfy and its enticements never deliver what they promise. In the end, only fellowship with God really satisfies. Too many people, however, find themselves slaves to their appetites.

Does the name Raynald ring a bell? Probably not. Actually, he was Raynald III, a fourteenth-century duke in an area that is now modern-day Belgium. Raynald loved to eat and was grotesquely overweight. As the story goes, there was a revolt in the kingdom led by Raynald's younger brother. In custody,

Raynald had a prison cell built around him. The room had no bars on the windows. It did not even have a lock on the door, which was built slightly smaller than normal.

The younger brother chided Raynald, informing him that any time he chose, he could come out and receive his crown and position back. All Raynald had to do was go on a self-enforced diet, walk out, and claim his throne. His brother even offered to restore his title and wealth as soon as he left the room.

Yet, the younger brother knew Raynald's weakness. He loved food. So each day, the younger brother had delivered to the elder a sumptuous variety of delicacies. And Raynald continued to gain weight, a prisoner not of locks and bars, but his own appetite.[3] What Raynald would never do was disengage from his appetite, which the apostle John identifies as an integral part of living in "the world."

And for our prodigal, it took the intervention of God to bring about the circumstances that would assist him to disengage from the world. How about you? Do you have any entanglements with the world that create for you a constant drain spiritually? Like the prodigal, I advise you, too, to disengage. So we find our prodigal friend off and running.

In practical terms this may mean not reading the magazines you used to read, or seeing the kind of movies you used to watch. It may mean breaking off with your friends at happy hour, or just monitoring what you watch on television. It may necessitate changing the kind of music you listen to, quitting your job, or even leaving the city where you live. Whatever it is that exercises an undue ungodly influence on you, it is best to leave it behind! Jesus said the prodigal son "arose." So should we. Yet, there are times when we really need some help.

Although our prodigal friend, to our knowledge, received no assistance other than the offer to help spend his money by his party friends, or of subsistence employment by the hog master, it would have been wonderful if he had had someone to lean on. How might it have been different if his older

brother, moved with concern, had gone searching for him? Or
if the father had sent a trusted servant? "Leave them alone and
they will come home" worked for Little Bo-Peep's sheep, but
it was not necessarily a working scenario for our prodigal.

When we are making our journey back to fellowship with
God, there are times when we need encouragement. Our men
who have attended Promise Keepers are learning how important it is to have brothers who will hold us accountable.
Many times we need people who love us to give us feedback,
provide insight, and help identify blind spots in our lives.
Sometimes we need help in reprogramming our emotions or
rebuilding right ideas in our minds.

My wife, Fern, is my biggest encourager and source of
feedback and insight. Apart from salvation, God's greatest
gift to a man is his wife. The foolish man refuses to listen to
her insights. The best example in the Bible of a man who foolishly refused to listen to his wife's advice was Pontius Pilate,
who ignored his wife's advice to have nothing to do with Jesus
at the time of His inquisition and crucifixion.[4]

There are times as people begin to walk afresh in the ways
of the Lord that they will need someone to pray with them
and encourage them along the way. If you have a good
Christian friend, or a Sunday school teacher, or a minister
who can help you, do not be afraid to ask for help. They cannot read your mind.

Solomon pointed out the principle that "as iron sharpens
iron, so a man sharpens the countenance of his friends." He
also said, "He who walks with wise men will be wise, but the
companion of fools will be destroyed." The apostle Paul
warned, "Do not be deceived: Evil company corrupts good
habits."[5] Friendships go both ways. They can help or they can
hinder. Be careful to get help when needed. But be sure that
the advice and encouragement you get is rooted in godly wisdom. I have a group of godly men I meet with regularly both
in small groups and one-on-one. Their counsel to me has been
invaluable.

At this point, our prodigal friend is approaching home. Having disengaged from the world and really needing help that never came, nonetheless he struggled onward. When he arrived, what kind of reception awaited him?

7

RECEPTION

How Thou canst think so well of us,
And be the God Thou art,
Is darkness to my intellect,
But sunshine to my heart.

—Author Unknown

God loves each of us as if there were only one of us.

—Augustine

The love of God is one of the great realities of the universe,
a pillar upon which the hope of the world rests.

—Author Unknown

"And he arose and came to his father. But when he was still a
great way off, his father saw him and had compassion, and ran
and fell on his neck and kissed him."

—Luke 15:20

THE JOURNEY IS ALMOST OVER. One more hill to climb. One more bend in the road and then the old homestead will come into sight. The closer our prodigal gets to home the greater his fear. Inside there is a voice that reverberates even more loudly: "You fool! They don't want you back! You are history! You're wasting your time! What a failure! You must be crazy! There is no way they could want you back after all you did!"

Yet at the very same time there is a glimmer of hope couched in the humility of a broken life. And there is confidence in the character of the father left behind. Ignoring the pain of his world-weary body, our prodigal rehearses his lines over and over in desperate hope that he will be granted an audience with his father.

"Father, I have sinned against heaven and before you, and I am no longer worthy to be called your son. Make me like one of your hired servants."[1]

His head hung low in near exhaustion, our bone-tired traveler approached home with a dread far greater than he had ever imagined. It was a moment of truth. There was no place else to go. He was out of options.

Rejection is a terrible experience and its pain is often beyond description. My wife, Fern, has lived with rejection all of her adult life. Unlike myself, Fern was not raised going to Sunday school but to the Temple. She comes from a Jewish home. Grandparents on both sides of her family were refugees to the States just after the turn of the century. The Statue of Liberty and Ellis Island were symbols of hope for refugees of Eastern Europe's terrible oppression of the Jews. The pogroms of Russia and Poland left emotional and physical scars way before Hitler began his assault on God's chosen.

Even before World War II, Fern's grandfather traveled to what eventually became the land of Israel and in its fledgling status helped to establish it as a nation. He was present even before the white flag of Israel with its blue border and star of David was raised for the first time in almost two thousand years. For him, God's people were finally at long last coming home. During that era when he fought for the independence of Israel, he contracted malaria and doctors advised him to travel on to the States. From there, this Orthodox gentleman who attended Shul faithfully every day of his life would support Israel as much as possible from across the Atlantic.

When Fern was seventeen years old, she heard the story of Jesus the Messiah, His love, His sacrificial death, and His miraculous resurrection. She heard of His willingness and ability to forgive her sins, and in the privacy of her bedroom one spring afternoon she surrendered her life to Jesus Christ. A key reason, I believe, was that she saw a difference in the lives of us who claimed to know Him. From that time to now her life has never been the same.

The news of Fern's conversion to Christianity did not sit well with her family. In fact, upon hearing the news, Fern's grandfather never spoke to her again. From that day until his death he refused to acknowledge her existence. In his mind, she was dead. To make the transition from first grandchild of great favor to patent rejection was very painful for Fern. It was painful for me to observe. No one likes rejection!

And the prodigal is now faced with the possibility of the realization of his greatest fear. The fear that after coming home, he too, would be rejected!

Many people have the notion that God is strictly a God of judgment, righteousness, and wrath. And there is an over-whelming sense that He is impossible to please, so why bother? Because of a multitude of warped ideas, many people feel that being accepted by God is an absolute impossibility and by default they consign themselves to the mass of people Paul described as "having no hope and without God in the world."[2]

As our prodigal friend turned up the lane walking to his father's house, something very unusual, very unsophisticated, and very wonderful occurred. We discover, in the actions of the father, the next step in the shortest way back to fellowship with God.

Step Four—Never Doubt God's Unconditional Love for You

Little did our prodigal know the endless hours of the father's agony on his behalf. Sleepless nights were filled with a mixture of prayer and worry. A heart with an empty place that only his lost son could fill refused to be consoled. Day in and day out the father's desperation grew. At the point of near paralysis, the old gray-haired man would sit and stare for hours on the front porch in that old rocker. Maybe today.

Maybe tomorrow. "Oh, God, bring my boy home" was his constant prayer. Was he an old fool who refused to concede to the obvious? Maybe so. Maybe not.

Days turned to weeks, weeks turned to months, and still no son. The seasons changed but still no word . . . and no son. Almost at the point of despair, one afternoon the old man looked down the lane and saw a familiar gait in the distance. "My eyes must be playing tricks on me," he told himself. But no. Could it be him? That disheveled man in the distance did look familiar. Could it be that God Almighty had heard and answered his prayers?

Suddenly something very strange and very wonderful occurred. The old man gathered up his robe and began to run in the direction of the wayward son. I say strange because old men in their dignity did not carry on like this. Yet, the old man is running, arms open wide in the direction of that wayward son come home. The father's hair is a little grayer and thinner. The lines in his face are etched deeper from the pain of bygone days. And now the tears have begun to flow. Tears of joy. Tears of relief. Tears of love. The impossible has become reality.

The boy is finally home. Gone is the smug self-sufficiency. Gone is the cocky attitude. Gone is the self-indulgent drive to experience the world. The weary traveler in great disgrace and profound humility has come home. Yet the father, overlooking the transgressions of past mistakes, seems oblivious to the sin. Why? Because he who was lost is now home.

At this point, Jesus teaches us a profound lesson. The old man represents the heart of Almighty God. If you have ever wondered what God is like, look long and hard at this image from the lips of the Savior. The father has one thing on his mind—my child is home.

If you have ever doubted the love of God for you, look closely at this picture. If you have reservations that maybe you have sinned too greatly to come back into fellowship, meditate on this. I am telling you that God feels the exact same way about you that this father felt about his wayward son. He loves you and longs for you to come home. He desires for you to enter again into fellowship with Him!

How much does God love you? God loved you enough to send Jesus to this earth to die in your place. The cross pictures for all of us the extent of God's love. Absolute and sacrificial is His love for you! For God so loved the world . . . and you in particular. Never doubt God's unconditional love for you!

For the prodigal, Jesus related, "But when he was still a great way off, his father saw him and had compassion, and ran and fell on his neck and kissed him." Any doubts? Welcome home!

I love the story told by George Will. It seems that Babe Ruth was at bat while Umpire Babe Pinelli called balls and strikes from behind the plate. The pitcher gets his signal, rocks, and fires. Ruth swings and misses. "Strike one," Pinelli yells. The Babe steps back in. The pitch is delivered, and again Ruth takes a mighty swing . . . and misses. "Strike two," says Pinelli. With that, Babe Ruth digs in for the next pitch. The pitcher winds up and delivers. Ruth does not move. From behind home plate Pinelli cries, "Strike three, the batter's out." Babe Ruth gets in Pinelli's face and says, "There's 40,000 people here who know that last one was a ball, tomato head." Pinelli looks around at the stadium full of people, then looks back to Ruth. "Maybe so," he says, "but mine is the only opinion that counts. The batter's out!"[3]

Not everyone was happy with the prodigal's return. Some might have argued that it was not fair to let him come home. Yet, similar to Babe Pinelli's, God's opinion is the only one that matters. Welcome home!

8

RESTORATION

The truth about man is that he needs to be loved the most when he deserves it the least.
—Author Unknown

There is no human wreckage, lying in the ooze of the deepest sea of iniquity, that God's deep love cannot reach and redeem.
—John Henry Jowett

"And the son said to him, 'Father, I have sinned against heaven and in your sight, and am no longer worthy to be called your son.' But the father said to his servants, 'Bring out the best robe and put it on him, and put a ring on his hand and sandals on his feet.'"
—Luke 15:21–22

NO SOONER HAD THE FATHER put his arms around his wayward son than the boy launched into his rehearsed petition. The preoccupation with his own self-importance now vanquished by his graduation from the school of hard knocks, he blurted out, "I have sinned against heaven and in your sight, and am no longer worthy to be called your son." Oswald Chambers brought light to this confession when he said, "Repentance does not cause a sense of sin—it causes a sense of inexpressible unworthiness."[1]

The prodigal's confession was truth in its purest form. He had sinned against God. Ultimately, all sin is first and foremost against God. That truth is revealed in King David's great confession, "Against You, You only, have I sinned, and done this evil in your sight."[2] Yet, for our prodigal friend, sin was also committed against his father. And this, too, he freely admitted.

The son squandered resources of time and money. He no doubt damaged the family's business, not to mention its reputation. His unrestrained lifestyle probably created a morale problem among the servants and had an even greater impact on his older brother. His actions left unseen scars on the old man. Yes, he had sinned in his father's sight.

In his own abject poverty of spirit, the prodigal unashamedly acknowledges, "I am no longer worthy to be called your son." Truer words were never spoken.

Yet, the old man does not relate to him in accordance with laws of right and wrong. "An eye for an eye" mentality does not factor here. Rather, his father relates to him in accordance with love, grace, and mercy.

Our Heavenly Father relates to us the same way. His love pursues us and receives us. His grace covers and compensates for our rebellion. His mercy triumphs over judgment. The words of the old hymn from a bygone era still ring true, "Jesus paid it all, all to Him I owe, sin had left a crimson stain, He washed it white as snow." God treats us with mercy because Jesus paid the penalty for our sins. That is why the apostle Paul declared that He is both "just and the justifier of the one who has faith in Jesus."[3]

Look closely at the old man's actions. Hear his words. Understand his heart. "Bring out the best robe and put it on him, and put a ring on his hand and sandals on his feet." A robe, a ring, and sandals communicate one thing. Here is a son, not a servant. Did he deserve such royal treatment? Certainly not! Did he expect it? No way! In his own words, our prodigal friend freely admitted, "I am no longer worthy to be called your son." Yet for all his failures, his father saw only a son come home.

When you take the steps to return to fellowship with God, He receives you the same way.

Step Five—Give and Request Forgiveness

Picture in your mind the cross of Christ. Notice that it consists of two beams, one vertical, the other horizontal. Use that as a depiction of the cross's ultimate intention—for you to be rightly related to your Heavenly Father and in turn be rightly related to your fellowman.

Our prodigal friend, having made his peace with God, has now ventured home to renew the lost fellowship and repair the damaged relationship with his father. This leads to the next step on our way back to fellowship with God. It addresses the issues surrounding forgiveness in the horizontal dimension, that is, getting broken relationships repaired. For this to be accomplished we must be willing to both grant and ask for forgiveness.

Granting Forgiveness

When Jesus concluded teaching His disciples what we call the Lord's Prayer, or Model Prayer, He shared a very stern warning:

> For if you forgive men their trespasses, your
> Heavenly Father will also forgive you. But if you do
> not forgive men their trespasses, neither will your
> Father forgive your trespasses.[4]

The refusal to forgive prohibits God from forgiving us. Conversely, if we are willing to forgive, it frees God to forgive us. Yes, the vertical is connected to the horizontal. They connect at the point of forgiveness. And the responsibility for choosing is in our hands.

At my church, we had the privilege of having Wellington Boone as our pulpit guest. Wellington's theme the night before at the Atlanta Promise Keepers Conference was reconciliation. When relationships are broken, they need to be reconciled. Racial reconciliation, as you may know, is a major emphasis for the men of Promise Keepers.

During the invitation time of our service, several people requested to share testimonies. One was a young lady named

Kay. Several years before she had endured a messy divorce. She felt abandoned, betrayed, and humiliated. She felt very foolish for having trusted her faithless husband. Now she was alone. And as a result, she had built up a tremendous reservoir of hatred and bitterness.

As Kay began to share, she related that her past bad experience had resulted in a blanket hatred of all men. As she expressed her sorrow for the pent-up anger and resulting hatred, I discerned that "all men" was not the root of her hatred. So I told her, in front of the entire congregation, that she was still angry with her ex-husband and her deepest need was to forgive him.

I agreed with her that what he did was terribly wrong and that he probably did not deserve to be forgiven. It is obvious, I said, that you do not *feel* like forgiving him. I went on to explain, however, that forgiveness is not a feeling but a choice, and I asked her if she would choose to forgive the one who had hurt her so deeply. After a few moments of hesitation, she said yes. And at that moment, tears streaming down her cheeks, Kay was finally released from the prison of bitterness.

Bitterness is internalized anger and is the result of being hurt and then refusing to forgive. Years ago I heard the saying that "Bitterness does more damage to the vessel in which it is stored than to anyone upon which it is poured." How true. It was eating Kay alive. But now, finally, she is free.

Although, to our knowledge, this was not our prodigal friend's problem, for many other prodigals it is. And many a person has been banished to the far country because of his or her own unwillingness to forgive. Upon closer look, however, our prodigal's run to the far country may have been partly motivated by his hatred for his older brother. Perhaps the same attitude displayed by the older brother upon the younger's return was present before his departure.

Is there anyone in your life whom you have been unwilling to forgive? If so, I urge you to make that choice immediately.

Life is too short and fellowship with God is too important to
trade them for bitterness and unforgiveness.

I love the testimony of "Blessed in California" as she
related her experience in "Dear Abby."

> Dear Abby: You asked what comforted readers
> when they were confronted with tragedy:
> Several years ago, my husband was on jury duty.
> When I found out that he had had an affair with one
> of the women jurors, I was devastated.
> We had three teen-aged children, and he had been
> the light of my life, and now he had betrayed me.
> As I sat thinking about it, it was as though God
> was asking me, "Who do you think you are, putting
> limits on my love? My son died on the cross for your
> sins and also for the sin your husband committed. If I
> can forgive him, you can, too."
> I replied, "Yes, Lord, I will forgive him." Then a
> sudden peace that I cannot explain settled over me.
> This year we will celebrate our 37th wedding
> anniversary. I am signing my name, but if you publish
> this, please sign me . . . BLESSED IN CALIFORNIA.[5]

Requesting Forgiveness

At other times the horizontal dimension of human relationships is damaged not by what someone has done to us,
but by what we did to, or failed to do for, someone else. And
we are at fault. Such was the case with our prodigal friend.
He was wrong, and we see him attempting successfully to
right the wrong.

Not too long ago, a young man who was both energetic
and intense came to see me. His name was Mark. He
explained how for a number of years he had worked for a
major corporation and had this past year made a career move
to another company. In his move, however, there had been
one unresolved point of contention. It had to do with his last
supervisor at the corporation. Quite frankly, Mark admitted,

he had resisted the supervisor's leadership due to the man's insensitivity and habit of using and discarding people. "The man was not right," Mark related, "but neither was I." Mark had departed with unresolved conflict and an attitude of insubordination. "What do I need to do?" he asked.

My advice to Mark was to see the man face-to-face. "When you meet with him, do not attempt to justify any-thing," I said. Tell him that your attitude was wrong. Tell him you are sorry. Ask him to forgive you. I warned Mark of the trap of balancing his own guilt (I did what was wrong and am convicted by it) and blame (but it is his fault). I instructed him to choose to forgive anything that was blamable before the meeting, and address strictly the issue of his own need for for-giveness.

I cautioned Mark that the man may very well rebuff his attempts but then quickly assured him that the substantive issue is his own willingness to right the wrong. Whether the man forgives you or not is not the important point. What is critical is your willingness to initiate the process. In going, I said, you are doing the right thing. You are obeying God and that is really the only thing that matters.

Knowing it is easy to back out of doing something like this, I asked Mark to let me know what happened. It was a form of accountability for him. If he had to face me, it would be easier to go through with it. He did.

Mark told me the man responded as he anticipated. Yet even though the former supervisor did not say, "I forgive you," the fact that Mark attempted to make things right was tremendously liberating.

On the human level, it is in the asking and not the receiv-ing that we are freed to enter into fellowship with God. The responsiveness to our initiative, or the lack of it, must be left in the hands of God. We cannot control and need not be held in bondage to another's unwillingness to forgive. Our respon-sibility is to ask. Yet, it is even better when we are successful and have "gained our brother."[6]

Coupled with the need to forgive and to request forgiveness is a similar issue. In Jesus' words, "The second is like unto it." There are times when simply asking for forgiveness is not enough. We must be willing to make restitution. Usually this is viewed as paying back what was owed to another. The classic biblical example of this is found in the story of Zacchaeus.

Zacchaeus was a tax collector. In Jesus' day tax collectors were notorious for taking advantage of people. They over-charged taxes and dared people to complain. After all, they were backed up by the Roman government. Fighting with them was futile. So Zacchaeus grew wealthy. Upon his con-version, Zacchaeus demonstrated his change of heart by announcing, "Look, Lord, I give half of my goods to the poor; and if I have taken anything from anyone by false accu-sation [common for tax collectors], I restore fourfold."[7] The point was, he made restitution for what he wrongly took.

When we are taking the shortest way back to fellowship with God, it is important that we make restitution where nec-essary. This may involve fulfilling unkept promises, paying unpaid debts, or owning up to secret sins. You know, those secret things you got away with but cannot forget. Permit me to relate a personal experience.

It was the spring of 1978 in Fort Worth, Texas. For those graduating with their masters and having aspirations for higher learning, it was time for prelims at Southwestern Seminary. This exercise involved several days of comprehen-sive examinations lasting from early morning until late in the afternoon. It was a draining experience, to say the least.

As the examination proceeded, I inadvertently saw the page of the person sitting next to me . . . and an answer. I argued with myself. "Go ahead and write it down. No, it was not your answer. Oh, go ahead." Because time was of the essence, and I knew no one knew, and I might have guessed and gotten it anyway, I wrote it down and went on. No big deal.

I had one problem. It was not my answer. The Lord peri-odically reminded me of that. I would tell myself it was a

little thing. Forget it! But I could not. Any sin big enough for
the Lord to keep bringing to your attention is a sin that must
be dealt with. Finally, I made an appointment with
Dr. Robert A. Baker, who had had responsibilities for admin-
istering the examination. Face-to-face I told him what had
happened and how I regretted it. I told him I was willing to
pay whatever penalty he thought necessary. In fact, I was
prepared to be dismissed from the Ph.D. program if that was
what he deemed appropriate.

Thinking back on the exams, Dr. Baker related that I had
done very well in that year's class of entrants, that it was an
insignificant infraction, and that I was forgiven. He told me
to forget about it and go home. I did.

Yet in that experience I learned a very painful lesson. You
cannot pull anything over on the Holy Spirit, so you might as
well be ruthlessly honest in your dealings. What if I had not
been willing to make amends? I guess I would have had to be
content living outside of fellowship with God. You see, in
many cases it is the little things the devil uses to create a
wedge between us and God. Friend, it is not worth it! If restitution is the order of the day, then do whatever it takes.

There are times when we cannot undo what we have done.
As the saying goes, "You cannot unscramble an egg." Yet, if
we are going to get back into fellowship with God, we must
be willing to forgive, request forgiveness, and make restitution! On the human level, these are the keys to restoration.

As you worked through your sin list earlier, it may be there
were some items you included that demanded steps of reconciliation—forgiving, requesting forgiveness, or making restitution. When these issues are settled and you have dealt
thoroughly with them, it is time to destroy the list and thank
God for His cleansing power. The apostle John declared,
"The blood [looking back to the sacrifice of Jesus on the
cross] of Jesus Christ His Son cleanses us from all sin."[8]

9

REJOICING

Joy is the serious business of Heaven.
—C. S. Lewis

Joy is not the absence of trouble but the presence of Christ.
—William Vander Haven

When I met Christ, I felt that I had swallowed sunshine.
—E. Stanley Jones

"And bring the fatted calf here and kill it, and let us eat and be merry; for this my son was dead and is alive again; he was lost and is found. And they began to be merry."
—Luke 15:23–24

CAN YOU IMAGINE THE EXCITEMENT as the word spread through the household and community that the prodigal had come home? "How did the old man treat that boy?" some might have asked. "As though he had never left," came the surprising response, to paraphrase Abraham Lincoln. The order of the day was barbecue and celebration. After all, to use the father's words, "This my son was dead and is alive again; he was lost and is found."[1]

Please notice that the prime mover in this atmosphere of rejoicing is the father. He has set the stage. It is his attitude of joy that prevails. Notice, too, that it is the father's joy into which the son and everyone else is invited to enter.

Embedded here is both a picture and a principle. The picture is one of joyful reunion. The principle is that fellowship with God produces joy. Recall King David's penitential prayer, "Restore to me the joy of Your salvation."[2]

When a child who has been estranged from the heart of his or her Heavenly Father comes home, the result is incredible joy—for both the Father and the child. In fact, joy is a by-product of entering and remaining in fellowship with God.

At this point, I believe it is important to make a distinction between joy and happiness. In our Declaration of Independence penned by Thomas Jefferson and formally adopted on July 4, 1776, we find these words:

> We hold these truths to be self-evident, that all
> men are created equal. That they are endowed by
> their Creator with certain inalienable rights, that
> among these are life, liberty, and the pursuit of happi-
> ness. . . .[3]

It has been said that Americans have been pursuing happiness ever since. Yet, if the truth be known, pursuing happiness is a perennial human endeavor.

Happiness depends on what happens. It is circumstance-oriented. When circumstances are favorable, we are happy. If not, we are unhappy. In the apostle Paul's words, it depends on "walking by sight," oriented to the circumstances we can see. Joy, however, is different.

Joy is a deep-seated contentment and security rooted in our relationship to our Heavenly Father. It comes through Jesus Christ and is produced in us by the Holy Spirit. It is not dependent on circumstances; rather, it transcends our circumstances. We can experience joy in spite of circumstances. In fact, joy disengages us from the roller coaster ride of happiness-oriented feelings. Discovering and living out this truth is the next step in the shortest way back to full fellowship with God.

Step Six—Rejoice in Your Restored Fellowship

In short order, happiness depends on what happens. It is circumstance- and sight-oriented. Joy, in contrast, depends on Jesus Christ and is faith-oriented. Your Heavenly Father's intention is that you discover joy as a daily experience. In fact, I believe joy is every believer's birthright, including yours.

One of my mentors was a professor of evangelism named Oscar Thompson. In the late 1970s I graded for him and as a result was given some quality time with this precious man of God. During those days I watched him slowly die of a very painful bone cancer. I can recall sitting in his office. As tears streamed down his face, he confessed that he felt like his foot was in a bucket of fire. His pain was excruciating. Yet, at the very same time, he related to me he had an incredible joy knowing that both his life and circumstances were in the hands of his loving Heavenly Father. He was one man, I am convinced, who had discovered the secret of joy.

The concern, for me, is how can you and I experience this same joy? The source of joy, of course, is the Lord. Jesus said, "These things I have spoken to you, that My joy may remain in you, and that your joy may be full."[4] So, the issue is, how is it supplied?

Joy, the Bible teaches, is part of the fruit of the Spirit, which means it is produced in us by God's Holy Spirit. It is a by-product of a life that is filled with the Holy Spirit; that is, a life lived under the Spirit's control.[5] This I equate with being in fellowship with God. Very simply, it is a life of trusting dependence.

The great devotional writer, Oswald Chambers, brought this into focus when he said:

> The one great challenge is this—do I know my
> risen Lord? Do I know the power of His indwelling
> Spirit? Am I wise enough in God's sight, but foolish
> enough according to the wisdom of the world, to
> trust in what Jesus said?[6]

Chambers says later:

> Any problem that comes while I obey God (and
> there will be many) increases my overjoyed delight,
> because I know that my Father knows and cares, and
> I can watch and anticipate how He will unravel my
> problems.[7]

Very simply, joy is produced in me by God's Spirit as I trust
Him with every detail of my life.

How can this joy be sustained? I believe it is cultivated in
us essentially by the attitude we choose when we place our
confidence in God. This confidence was displayed in the life
of the Old Testament hero, Joseph, who at the culmination
of a life of betrayal at the hands of his brothers could look
back and conclude, "But as for you, you meant evil against
me; but God meant it for good, in order to bring it about as
it is this day, to save many people alive."[8] Joseph could not
choose his circumstances. What he could choose, however,
was his attitude toward them. And his attitude was this: "No
matter what happens, I am placing my confidence in God's
faithfulness."

I want to encourage you and say to you that this joy can
be yours no matter how long or how little you have been a
believer. In fact, it does not depend on where you are so much
as in what direction you are moving. As long as you are moving closer to God, joy is the order of the day. That is why
someone like my friend James, who has been a Christian for
a short time (he was miraculously delivered from a life of
organized crime), can have incredible joy, while (and in contrast) some people who have been believers for years (but are
oriented toward their circumstances and therefore somewhat
cynical) live joyless lives. One looks at circumstances; the
other focuses on God.

How about you? Where is your focus? The choice is yours.

More specifically, joy is the result of a simple childlike
confidence in God's sovereignty. It is that attitude that confesses "I know God is in control of everything even if my

apparent circumstances do not confirm it." It is trusting in the all-powerful, all-knowing, ever-present Lord, even when we do not feel like it.

It is the "will to trust" winning out over the "feeling to doubt." It is you choosing faith over sight and trusting God in spite of the circumstances. It is finally resting on the apostle Paul's declaration, "And we know that all things work together for good to those who love God, to those who are the called according to His purpose."[9] It is even saying in the midst of heartbreak, "Lord, I am trusting you." It really is your choice.

The question running through your mind (and I admit it has run through mine often) may be this, is God really sovereign? Or is that just a theological concept from some ancient theologian who thought it sounded good? Should we not rather accept Harold Kushner's conclusion in *When Bad Things Happen to Good People* that in the end God really is powerless to do much of anything constructive, much less intervene in the affairs of mankind? To swallow that one is a major step in the wrong direction. In fact it loops you back to walking by sight and not by faith. It consigns you to the ranks of those who are tyrannized by their circumstances.

I believe there are times when the Lord teaches us a truth mentally and then gives us an experience to verify its reality. For me that happened in late spring of 1983 in Fort Worth. The subject was the sovereignty of God.

I was visiting prospects on Saturday morning. If someone visited our church on the previous Sunday, I tried to contact them, preferably with a personal visit on the following Saturday. I had stopped by to visit one family, and upon finding no one home, left a note on the front door. Before I drove away, however, I did say hello to their next-door neighbors (members of our congregation) while they were working in their front yard.

While chatting for a few moments, another neighbor, Lonnie was his name, walked over. Lonnie was in the Air Force and stationed at Carswell Air Force Base. I asked

Lonnie about his family, if they attended church anywhere, and concluded with an invitation to visit Wedgwood, where I was pastor.

The next day, to my surprise, Lonnie, his wife, and children were in attendance. And the following Saturday morning, true to form, I found myself knocking at their door. Because they had friends in from out of town, I only intended to stay for a moment. I asked as I was leaving, however, if there was anything I could pray about for them.

At that moment Lonnie teared up and said, "Yes, there is one thing." He asked me to pray for his dad, who was dying of cancer and lost. I assured him I would and then asked if he was in a local hospital. Lonnie's answer was, "No, he's in Pittsburgh." A cold chill went up my spine.

"Lonnie," I asked, "do you know what I am doing tomorrow when the morning services are over?" I then related to him that I was catching a flight to the Southern Baptist Convention meeting in . . . Pittsburgh!

Lonnie quietly explained to me that his father, John, was in the McKeesport General Hospital's oncology wing in suburban Pittsburgh. I assured Lonnie that if it were possible I would see his father the following week.

Wednesday came and with it a break in our three-day annual business meeting. I asked David Cobb and my attorney friend, Oliver Miles, if they would go with me to McKeesport General. David, my associate pastor and one of my dearest friends in the world, drove his van while we talked strategy.

When we reached the hospital we found John just as Lonnie had said. We introduced ourselves, then David and Oliver stepped back (and prayed like crazy) while I talked. Before us was the emaciated body of a formerly hardworking, hard-living coal miner now consumed not only by cancer but also by fear. I learned later that he had died on the operating table about six months before during a heart operation and was terrified by what he saw on the other side. He was so fearful, I might add, that he would not allow anyone to turn off the lights of his room. And he constantly begged for someone to be with him.

I told John that I was a friend of Lonnie's and had promised him I would stop by and see his dad while in town on business. After a moment of small talk I related that his son was very concerned about him. Then I inquired, "May I ask you a personal question?" For me and him this was a moment of truth. He acquiesced, shaking his head affirmatively.

"Mr. Williams," I said, "I know you are a very sick man and I want to know—Are you ready to die?" With steel blue eyes that forever will be etched into my memory, he said very simply, "No!" Then I followed up by asking him if I might share with him how to prepare to die. Again, his answer was brief, "Yes." And I proceeded. I shared with him that God loved him, yet hated his sin. I explained to him how Jesus Christ had come to earth to die on the cross to take our punishment for sin and that anyone who desired could receive God's free gift of eternal life by simply receiving Jesus Christ as personal Savior through repentance and faith. By this time his tears were flowing unashamedly. I asked him if he wanted to invite Jesus into his heart to forgive and cleanse him. And he said, "Yes!" In that oncology wing of McKeeseport General Hospital on a warm late spring afternoon (June 16, 1983, to be exact), John Williams was born again. I left him a copy of Billy Graham's tract, "Steps to Peace with God" as a follow-up and departed after prayer. For the record, he died a few weeks later.

Before we left the hospital I called Lonnie in Fort Worth, sharing with him that his dad had just invited Jesus into his life. I believe I could have heard that shout all the way from Texas, with or without the telephone. To this day I look back at the miraculous sequence of events that led to John's salvation and my learning experientially about the sovereignty of God. Only God could have done that! If the Lord can sovereignly and supernaturally answer one man's heartfelt prayers for the salvation of his dad, He can certainly watch over the details of our lives.

Joy is the by-product of trusting a sovereign God with the circumstances of our lives. Fighting against this is the constant temptation to give in to the joy stealers. These include regret and unforgiveness from the past, worry, stress, fear, and grief. Any feeling that pulls you away from trusting God can steal your joy.

As I conclude this chapter on rejoicing, let me offer two verses of Scripture. They come from the pen of King Solomon. He wrote,

> Trust in the Lord with all your heart,
> And lean not on your own understanding;
> In all your ways acknowledge Him,
> And He shall direct your paths.[10]

Here is the promise that God will guide you. If I know that He is in control of my life, I have peace and joy. This promise is for every believer!

Perhaps you have been struggling with this issue of joy. Let me share with you what Jesus said to His disciples after they exercised supernatural power. He said, "Nevertheless, do not rejoice in this, that the spirits are subject to you, but rather rejoice because your names are written in heaven."[11] Ultimately, we experience joy when we comprehend that we are, indeed, children of the Living God!

Like the prodigal son who returned to his father, we too can experience the joy of renewed fellowship with our Heavenly Father.

10

REBUILDING

You cannot stay where you are and go on with God.
—Henry Blackaby

It costs to follow Jesus Christ, but it costs more not to.
—Author Unknown

A disciple is a person who learns to live the life his teacher lives.
—Juan Carlos Ortiz

Discipleship is more than getting to know what the teacher knows. It is getting to be what he is.
—Juan Carlos Ortiz

"Now his older son was in the field. And as he came and drew near to the house, he heard music and dancing. So he called one of the servants and asked what these things meant. And he said to him, 'Your brother has come, and because he has received him safe and sound, your father has killed the fatted calf.'"
—Luke 15:25–27

NO DOUBT THE PRODIGAL'S RETURN generated considerable turmoil. For the older brother, especially, the younger brother's homecoming was not a source of joy but of jealousy. In fact, the prodigal's return was viewed with severe suspicion. And rightly so. Had he not indulged in a long list of forbidden activities? Had he not betrayed the family? Had he not disgraced his father?

At this point, I want to isolate a key issue. When we have been away from God and we now desire to start over, how can we ensure we will not backslide? Can we be trusted? People will be watching us, thinking, *It will never last.* Or perhaps we will lack confidence and in the back of our own minds we will think, "It's just a matter of time before I mess up again." What can we do to ensure that will not be the case?

Step Seven—Rebuild Broken Walls of Behavior and Belief

Several years ago I was out on my morning run. That particular day I had decided to jog from my home to the bridge over the Cumberland River and back. The eight-mile route was primarily on Old Hickory Boulevard, a pretty heavily trafficked thoroughfare with nice sidewalks most of the way.

In the second mile of the run I looked with horror as a full-grown German shepherd was coming seemingly out of nowhere with fangs bared to attack. Having almost no time to prepare, I tensed up as I prepared for the inevitable.

When the dog was only a foot or so from me, something wonderful happened—it reached the end of its leash. In the midst of a terrifying leap in my direction, the dog ran out of chain and was momentarily suspended in air. I will never forget the overwhelming sense of relief or the lesson I learned.

The dog was territorial and, as such, its owner had given it freedom to run in its yard. In fact, the leash permitted it access to most of the private property. Its boundary ended at the edge of the sidewalk, which was public property. As long as I stayed on the sidewalk, I was safe. If I had ventured onto the dog's turf, however, I would have had a major problem.

Picture if you would an imaginary fence along the edge of the sidewalk. As long as I stayed on the sidewalk I was safe. If I stepped off the sidewalk, I was in trouble. In a similar manner, God has told us in the Bible how we should live. The Bible often identifies this as our "walk." As long as we walk within the boundaries God has established for us, we will be safe. If, however, we venture outside the God-ordained boundaries, we can expect to be attacked with destructive temptation. As long as our prodigal friend remained within the confines of his father's boundaries, he was safe. When he departed, he was on his own.

As believers, certain behaviors are off-limits to us. In fact, often a single besetting sin will cause a believer to stumble repeatedly. If you have a weakness, I guarantee the devil will exploit it. I have seen believers struggle with alcohol, drugs, immorality of various forms, addictions to gambling, dishonesty, greed, gossip, procrastination, outbursts of anger, pride, and many more flaws.

I counsel believers to build mental walls of behavior, certain parameters outside of which they will not venture, especially in areas where sin in times past has had a stronghold. In the words of the Apostle Paul, "Make no provision for the flesh, to fulfill its lusts."[1] As believers, there are some places we will not go, some things we will not do, and some crowds with whom we will not run.

Too often, temptation comes as a combination of an unexpected opportunity and an unguarded heart. I believe the great Old Testament personality, Daniel, learned the secret of withstanding temptation. The Scripture records that, "He purposed in his heart that he would not defile himself . . ."[2] That is, he decided ahead of time that if a certain temptation came, he already had made up his mind and the answer was "no!"

We, too, must build those mental walls of acceptable behavior where we decide ahead of time that certain activities are strictly off-limits. And we must ruthlessly refuse even to flirt with them!

For the Christian, however, many times temptation will not come as a clearly defined daylight-and-dark issue. Often we are tempted in the gray areas of life where we are honestly not sure what is right and wrong. In those times, what should a believer do?

The apostle Paul knew it would be impossible to address every ethical issue confronting believers. So, in addition to certain moral certitudes, he provided believers with four behavioral principles. I believe these, too, can help you establish a set of behavioral guidelines. Here are the questions from Paul that I suggest you ask before becoming involved in any activity:

1. Is this activity helpful or profitable? That is, does any good come out of it?
2. Will this activity make me susceptible to any form of bondage?
3. Will this activity, if indulged in, cause another person, especially a believer, to stumble?
4. Will this activity bring glory to God?[3]

Let me encourage you to use these as fence posts in marking off your behavior as a believer.

In addition to constructing mental parameters of acceptable behavior, we must also work to build our relationship with our Heavenly Father. This involves a daily surrendering of our lives to allow Jesus Christ to be the boss of our lives, coupled with the willing submission to the Holy Spirit's leading.

Recently I was reading in my favorite journal and ran across the story told by author and business leader Fred Smith. He related:

> One of my treasured memories comes from a doughnut shop in Grand Saline, Texas. There was a young farm couple sitting at the table next to mine. He was wearing overalls and she a gingham dress. After finishing their doughnuts, he got up to pay the bill, and I noticed she didn't get up to follow him.
>
> But then he came back and stood in front of her. She put her arms around his neck, and he lifted her up, revealing that she was wearing a full-body brace. He lifted her out of her chair and backed out the

front door to the pickup truck, with her hanging from his neck.

As he gently put her into the truck, everyone in the shop watched. No one said anything until a waitress remarked, almost reverently, "He took his vows seriously."[4]

In a similar way, Jesus wants us to take our vows as Christians seriously.

I have discovered for myself two keys to growing in my relationship with God. First, I need a daily intake of Scripture. This involves reading the Bible, reflecting on its meaning and impact on my life, and then purposing in my heart to do what it says. In the Great Commission Jesus instructed His followers to teach disciples "to do whatsoever I have commanded you."[5]

It is not enough to *know*; we must be willing to *do*. The biblical writer James put it this way, "But be doers of the word, and not hearers only, deceiving yourselves."[6] In other words, if I hear but do not practice, I am deceived into thinking I am approved by God when, in fact, I am not.

The Apostle Paul made a very important point when, in his letter to young Timothy, he wrote,

> All Scripture is given by inspiration of God, and is profitable for doctrine, for reproof, for correction, for instruction in righteousness, that the man of God may be complete, thoroughly equipped for every good work.[7]

Here, Paul pointed out that the Bible is given for a purpose. It will provide doctrine, which is simply the teachings of Scripture. If you want to know the truth from God's perspective, here is where you will find it. Second, it will offer reproof; that is; it will point out for you where your life is outside of God's will—whether an action, attitude, or aspiration. Third, it will correct. In other words, it will teach you how to get right with God and correct what is wrong. Finally, it will instruct you in righteousness. The word *instruct* may more accurately be translated "train." It will show you how to discipline yourself, while depending on the Lord, in order to bring you to a place of spiritual maturity. That is why God gave us the Bible.

On my desk is a little paperweight. The base, made of white marble, is about the size of a deck of playing cards. Mounted to the base is a small metallic statue of a track shoe. I received this paperweight when I completed running the Dallas White Rock Marathon in December of 1978. Although I had run track in high school and had continued to run during college, I had never attempted a marathon.

No matter how badly I might have wanted to run a marathon up to that time, I was incapable of doing so. Why? I had not trained for it. And no amount of willpower could compensate for a lack of training. Four months before this race, however, a friend, Dr. Robert Paul Martin, gave me a training schedule out of *Runner's World* magazine. I began to follow the routines it prescribed, and by race day I was able to complete the race.

Even as *Runner's World* can be a runner's Bible in marathon training, so the Bible is given to train us for the race of life. If we will learn what it says and practice what we learn, we will discover ourselves developing in the matter of righteousness and spiritual maturity. One of the highlights of my day is when I rise early and read my Bible.

Let me remind you that having the training schedule and reviewing it daily did not train me for the marathon. It was *doing* what it said. The same is true for your Bible. Do not just read it—that is important. Do what it says!

Coupled with a steady intake of Scripture, I believe it is important for Christians to cultivate a consistent prayer life. This is the second key to rebuilding walls of belief. The Bible is filled with encouragement for us to pray, instruction on how to pray, and examples of people praying.

Jesus, in his Sermon on the Mount, gives to the disciples a Model Prayer.[8] In fact, the components and guidelines of the

prayer provide a healthy checklist of subjects for our prayers.
I want you to note first, however, Jesus' follow-up counsel on
prayer in that same address:

> Ask, and it will be given to you; seek, and you will
> find; knock, and it will be opened to you. For every-
> one who asks receives, and he who seeks finds, and to
> him who knocks it will be opened. Or what man is
> there among you who, if his son asks for bread, will
> give him a stone? Or if he asks for a fish, will he give
> him a serpent? If you then, being evil, know how to
> give good gifts to your children, how much more will
> your Father who is in Heaven give good things to
> those who ask Him![9]

Jesus is encouraging us to pray. He points out in broad
strokes how it is the Father's intention to answer our prayers!
It is his nature and character to answer!

He also instructs us on the "how-to" of praying. In the pas-
sage just cited, Jesus tells us that prayer first and foremost is
business between us and God. It is, therefore, to be motivated
from a desire to know God and not to be seen by people. He
promises that the Father who sees in secret will reward us
openly, assuring us that the Father knows our needs before we
ask. He then proceeds to instruct us in the components of
effective prayer: I remind you again of the importance of forgiveness to answered prayer.

Jesus gives the Model Prayer to us not so we can pray these
exact words but so we will have a model or basis for our
prayers. Powerful praying always begins with praise.
Matthew 6:9 says, "In this manner, therefore, pray: 'Our
Father in heaven, Hallowed be Your name.'" It begins with
praise. The word *hallowed* means reverent, sanctified, set
aside, or holy. It means we are understanding and acknowledging the awesome reality of the sovereign God. We are
coming into His presence acknowledging that He is special
and there is none like Him in all the earth or universe.

Praise is the great antidote for discouragement. Praise acknowledges who God is. Understand that we need to start our prayers with praise.

Jesus then talks about prioritizing, "Your kingdom come. Your will be done on earth as it is in heaven." Jesus says as you come into the presence of God and lift up praise to Him, you begin to realize who God is and who you are. We are actors on God's stage. He is not an actor on our stage. We are little people in our great big Heavenly Father's world. We need to understand that it is His concerns that come first. What we are saying is we want our Lord to be King in our hearts, and His will to be done in our lives, and our desire is that His will will be done throughout all the earth. Jesus returns to that principle after He warns us about worry and says, "Seek first the kingdom of God and His righteousness, and all these things shall be added to you."[10] God says that when you pray, begin with praise—understand who you are in relationship to Him. Then move to prioritizing, saying we want God's kingdom to come first and His will to be done— just as it is in heaven. We want it to be done on earth and in our lives. That is always a key for prayer. Answered prayer is a prayer prayed in the will of God. It is prayed from the heart of a person who seeks first the kingdom of God and His righteousness and then allows God to take care of everything else. Jesus taught us that we should put His interests above our own. That is where we start with prayer.

The third component deals with our provision. After we understand who God is and we praise Him and we understand that He and His kingdom come first, then we can begin to deal with our personal needs. He teaches us to pray, "Give us this day our daily bread." Jesus is not saying you can pray about bread and that is all you can pray for. That is not the point. *Daily bread* is a term that means my daily personal needs. It means every need I have. When we pray and address the issue of our provision, we are acknowledging that God is our provider, our sustainer, and everything that we have or hope to have or need comes from Him.

Some people would rather worry than trust God. That is exactly what Jesus is dealing with right here. I once saw a sign on an office wall that said, "I am going to have a nervous breakdown. I deserve it. I've worked hard for it." Sometimes that is the attitude people have. God says we do not have to feel that way. We need to understand that He has everything we need.

Some of us may find it hard to say we are trusting Him for our daily provision. Some live in nice homes, drive nice cars, have nice salaries and bank accounts and plenty of insurance. We have everything we could ever want. When we are provided for like that, sometimes it is difficult to say each day that we are trusting Him for our every need. It has to be a conscious decision. We have to realize that He blessed us in many ways but also realize it could all be gone with the snap of a finger.

I heard about a pastor who went to visit a wealthy widow. He walked inside her big house filled with antiques. She had more money than she knew what to do with. But her husband was dead. As she sat there and talked with the pastor, she said she would give everything she had for one more day with her husband. That puts life into perspective.

God wants us to acknowledge every day that we are trusting in Him for provision. For some this prayer is incredibly relevant. You live hand to mouth. Sometimes you do not know where the next meal is coming from or where your next job is coming from. You have it tough. Whether you have a lot or a little, God says He wants you to depend on Him for your daily provision.

The fourth component deals with pardon. It says, "Forgive us our debts, as we forgive our debtors." Jesus is not talking about financial debts. He is talking about moral indebtedness, such as if you have something against somebody or someone has something against you. Unforgiveness is probably the greatest reason for unanswered prayers today. If you want your prayers to be answered, you have to be willing to forgive those who hurt you, or offend you, or who have taken advantage of you.

He wants us to keep our sins confessed. Psalm 66:18 says if you regard iniquity in your heart the Lord is not going to hear your prayer. It does not say you are going to be lost again, but do not count on your prayers being answered. If we want to have powerful prayers, we need to have pure lives so our prayers can be answered. Jesus said to ask for pardon—"Lord, forgive me my debts as I forgive others."

Perhaps you heard the old story of the man who owned a carriage. He needed a new carriage driver. He was interviewing prospective drivers for his carriage. He asked each the same question. He told them they were going to have some very precious cargo. His family was going to be riding with them. He wanted to ask them something. Down the road was a dangerous drop-off, which fell a number of feet. He asked how close to that drop-off they could get before feeling unsafe. The first young man said he probably could get within a foot and a half of it before he would begin to feel uncomfortable. He was told he would not do. The second driver answered that he thought he could get within three feet of the edge before feeling there would be danger to the man's family. He also was told he was not needed. The third man answered that he did not want to find out. He was going to stay as far away from that drop-off as he could. He was hired.

Many times Christians play this game: "How close can I get to sin without neutralizing my effectiveness, or forfeiting my fellowship with God, or making a mess out of my life?" It is almost as if we want to go right up to the line. God says do not do that, but stay as far away from it as you can.

Sometimes I meet people I call injustice collectors. They remember anyone who has ever offended them, or hurt their feelings, or done anything, or taken anything away from them, in all their life. They can tell you all about it. It is as though they carry a great big bag of injustices on their shoulders. All you have to do is talk to them for about five minutes, and they will tell you about everybody who has ever offended them. That kind of person with that kind of attitude will never get his or her prayers answered. Jesus said, speaking to us about prayer, that we are to say, "Lord, forgive us our debts as we forgive our debtors." I believe Jesus is talking to believers here. I do not believe He is addressing the issue of judicial forgiveness from the penalty of sin. That comes when we place our faith in Christ. But He is making a distinction between acceptance and approval, between a relationship and fellowship. He is saying your approval and fellowship with God can be neutralized by unforgiveness or unconfessed sin.

A fifth component instructs us to pray for protection. Jesus said, "And do not lead us into temptation but deliver us from the evil one." Do you pray, "Lord, keep me out of trouble," or "Keep me away from temptation; do not let anything come my way that will cause me to stumble or to fall." I believe Christians ought to pray that way. Jesus understands where the rocks are under the water and where the mines are out in the field. He understands where the traps are that can trip us. We need to pray for Him to lead us away from those things. God is not going to tempt anybody. What Jesus is teaching is for us to ask the Lord to lead us away from temptation. Ask Him not to let us fall or stumble or make a mess out of things, but rather deliver us from the evil one.[11] The thrust is, "Lord, protect me!" That is a legitimate prayer.

The prayers for provision, pardon, and protection are for our benefit. If God already knows what we need anyway, why do we need to pray it? The principle is this: God knows and cares about us, but He wants us to tell Him our needs. He wants us to know what we need and pray for it.

The final component says, "For Yours is the kingdom and the power and the glory forever. Amen." Jesus is saying that everything begins and ends with God. This is an affirmation and acknowledgment of who God is. We are saying that if our prayers get answered, it is because God is the one who is answering them. He is the one who heard them and answered them. In my prayers, I always pray "in Jesus' name" because John 14:14 says, "If you will ask anything in My [Jesus'] name, I will do it." The point is not to add on "in Jesus name" as some magical incantation. We pray this because we want our prayers to be in line with the will and ways of God and for Jesus to be glorified in our lives.

Alfred Lord Tennyson once wrote, "More things are wrought by prayer than this world dreams of. Wherefore, let thy voice rise like a fountain, night and day."[12] What great advice!

The slave trader turned preacher, John Newton, put it this way,

> Thou art coming to a King,
> Large petitions with Thee bring,
> For His grace and power are such
> None can ever ask too much.[13]

The Bible is also filled with examples of people praying. Abraham prayed for a son. Moses prayed for God's guidance and mercy. Joshua prayed for discernment. David prayed for forgiveness. Solomon prayed for wisdom. Hannah prayed for a son. Elijah prayed for fire and rain. Daniel prayed for insight and wisdom. Esther, no doubt, prayed for courage. Jonah prayed for a second chance. The Bible records hundreds of prayers and hundreds of answers.

I am drawn particularly to the prayer of the celebrated figure, Jabez. Scripture recorded both the prayer and the answer:

> And Jabez called on the God of Israel saying, "Oh, that You would bless me indeed, and enlarge my territory, that Your hand would be with me, and that You would keep me from evil, that I may not cause pain!" So God granted him what he requested.[14]

My friend, if God will answer the prayer of Jabez, and a host of others, He will answer your prayers as well.

To recap, if we are going to remain in fellowship with God, we must rebuild walls of both behavior and belief. The latter is done, especially, as we have steady intake of God's Word and pray consistently. You can do this!

11

RECONNECTING

Faults are thick where love is thin.
—Author Unknown

*The loneliest place in the world is the human heart
when love is absent.*
—E. C. McKenzie

Love is not a feeling but a choice.
—Soren Kierkegaard

*"But he was angry and would not go in. Therefore his father came
out and pleaded with him. So he answered and said to his father,
'Lo, these many years I have been serving you; I never transgressed
your commandment at any time; and yet you never gave me a
young goat, that I might make merry with my friends. But as soon
as this son of yours came, who has devoured your livelihood with
harlots, you killed the fatted calf for him.' And he said to him, 'Son,
you are always with me, and all that I have is yours. It was right
that we should make merry and be glad, for your brother was
dead and is alive again, and was lost and is found.'"*
—Luke 15:28–32

WITH OUR PRODIGAL FRIEND safely at home and working on
rebuilding those mental walls of behavior and belief, there is
one final issue he must address. He needs to reconnect with
his family and community. No doubt he is marked as a problem personality, to say the least. And, specifically, his

relationship with his older brother demands first-class attention. Yet, it serves to draw out the importance of reestablish-
ing godly relationships across the board.

The English poet and cleric, John Donne, said it so elo-
quently when he wrote,

> No man is an island entire of itself; every man is a
> piece of the Continent, a part of the main; if a clod be
> washed away by the sea, Europe is less . . . ; any
> man's death diminishes me, because I am involved in
> mankind; and therefore never send to know for whom
> the bell tolls; it tolls for thee.[1]

Donne's assessment reminds us of the final step in return-
ing and maintaining fellowship with God.

Step Eight—Reconnect with and Reinforce Right Relationships

Donne's plea was for people to understand their intercon-
nectedness with others. If that is true with humanity in general, it is doubly true for the believer.

In a world where people are alienated and isolated from
others, and loneliness can at times be overwhelming, we must
understand that God has built in a relational safety net for
His children called the church. In fact, the Bible teaches that
when we become believers we become members of His body,
a metaphor for the church.

We live in a culture that encourages individualism. In some
respects this is good. But in one's spiritual life, the Christian
faith is intended to be lived in community. That community is
a local church.

Some people have argued that when we are saved we
become part of the universal church and conclude that is suf-
ficient. We are "numbered with those saints in glory" as the
old song goes. Yet, a close examination of Scripture clearly
mandates involvement in a local fellowship of believers. If
you are going to sustain your fellowship with the Father, it is
imperative that you become a part of a local church.

If you are looking for a church home, I offer these sugges-
tions. First, make sure it takes the Bible seriously. Also, be
sure it focuses on the importance of a personal relationship
with Jesus Christ. Third, observe to see if the people love one
another. And fourth, see if it is concerned about spreading the
message of salvation. If these four line up, you have a winner.

Let me caution you that the church is not the building; it
is the people who meet in the building. Never mistake the
church for bricks and mortar.

Some people have asked, "Why bother with church?" Let
me give you ten reasons.

First, God commands it. The Bible says, "Do not forsake
the assembling of yourselves together as is the habit of
some."[2] God thinks it is important for you to participate in a
local church.

Second, Christ died for it. When the apostle Paul is
addressing issues of marriage relationships he says,
"Husbands, love your wives, just as Christ also loved the
church and gave Himself for her."[3] How did Christ love the
church? He loved it sacrificially and absolutely. He loved it
enough to sacrifice His life for it. This tells me that Christ
placed an incredibly high value on the church.

Third, God has given the church the assignment to communicate the message of salvation to the entire world. In the
Great Commission, the church is instructed to "make disciples
of all the nations."[4] This is certainly a weighty responsibility.

Fourth, God has guaranteed that the church will not only
survive, but also it will thrive. In the retreat setting of
Caesarea Philippi, Jesus said to his disciples, "On this rock
[of Peter's confession that Jesus is the Son of God] I will build
My church, and the gates of Hades shall not prevail against
it."[5]

Fifth, it is with the church that we are invited to worship.
Jesus, talking with the Samaritan woman, said, "But the hour
is coming, and now is, when the true worshipers will worship
the Father in spirit and truth; for the Father is seeking such to
worship Him."[6]

Sixth, it is where we are cared for. Jesus said this to His disciples. "By this all will know that you are My disciples, if you have love for one another."[7] One of the identifying marks of the church is that its members care for one another. It is here you will be ministered to and cared for, especially in times of crises.

Seventh, it is where we learn. One of the identifying trademarks of the church is that it should be a learning community. The church has been given the responsibility for safeguarding and passing on, generation to generation, the truths of God's Word and how to apply them in day-to-day life.[8]

Eighth, it is where we are prepared to impact our world. The Bible teaches us that believers are to function in this world as catalysts for righteousness. We are equipped to do this as the church gathers.[9]

Ninth, in the church, our values are reinforced. With the world's constant attack on morality, it is here that the right values are taught and encouraged.[10]

Tenth, it is where families are strengthened. With all the stressors on the family today, the church is one place where the family and its accompanying values can be reinforced.

These are ten reasons for involvement in the church. With all of the negative influences in the world, one force standing against the moral landslide in our culture is the church. If you are going to maintain your fellowship with God, you need the encouragement that comes from being a part of a family of faith, a local church.

Perhaps you have been away from the Lord for a long time. And even now you are debating, Is it worth the effort? You will never be the person God created you to be as long as you are estranged from your Heavenly Father. My friend, you have no time to waste. Life is too short to throw it away on things that do not matter. If you are going to experience life as God intended, I encourage you now to begin your homeward journey back into fellowship with your Heavenly Father. You see, today is the only sure time you have to make

that decision. Let me leave you with what I consider a sobering thought.

> The clock of life is wound but once,
> And no man has the power,
> To tell just when the hands will stop,
> At late or early hour.
> Now is the only time we own;
> Give, love, toil with a will,
> And place no faith in tomorrow,
> For the clock may then be still.[11]

Endnotes

Chapter One, Restlessness
1. Genesis 3:1–19.
2. John 16:8–11.
3. *Leadership Journal,* 1993, Vol. 14:4, 56.
4. Daniel 1:8; 1 Corinthians 10:13.

Chapter Two, Rebellion
1. Hebrews 11:25.
2. Ben Franklin, *Great Thoughts,* 142.
3. Psalm 90:12.
4. Hebrews 13:5.

Chapter Three, Reversal
1. Psalm 106:15.
2. Joshua 7:1–26; 22:20; Numbers 32:23.
3. 2 Samuel 11:1–12:23.
4. Romans 2:4.
5. Judges 13:24f.
6. Judges 16:21.
7. Judges 16:22–31.
8. 1 Corinthians 11:30; Acts 5:1–11.
9. Hebrews 12:8.
10. 2 Corinthians 13:5.
11. Galatians 6:7.

Chapter Four, Regret
1. James 1:5–8.
2. Matthew 7:7–8.
3. Matthew 11:28–29.
4. John 16:8–11.
5. Romans 8:1.
6. John 8:36; 2 Corinthians 3:17.

Chapter Five, Repentance
1. 1 John 1:9; Proverbs 28:13.
2. Psalm 51:3–4.

Chapter Six, Return
1. John 3:16.
2. 1 John 2:15–16.
3. *Dynamic Preaching,* July 1990, 17.
4. Matthew 27:19–26.
5. Proverbs 27:17; 13:20; 1 Corinthians 15:33.

Chapter Seven, Reception
1. Luke 15:18–19.
2. Ephesians 2:12.
3. George Will, *Men at Work* (New York: Harper Perennial, 1991), 64.

Chapter Eight, Restoration
1. Oswald Chambers, *My Utmost for His Highest,* August 22.
2. Psalm 51:4.
3. Romans 3:26.
4. Matthew 6:14–15.
5. "Dear Abby," *The Tennessean,* 13 July 1995, 2D.
6. Matthew 18:15.
7. Luke 19:1–10.
8. 1 John 1:7.

Chapter Nine, Rejoicing
1. Abraham Lincoln in Gore Vidal, *Lincoln,* Luke 15:24.
2. Psalm 51:12.
3. Thomas Jefferson, *The Portable Thomas Jefferson,* 235.
4. John 15:11.
5. Galatians 5:22; Ephesians 5:18.
6. Oswald Chambers, October 27.
7. Ibid., December 14.
8. Genesis 50:20–21.
9. Romans 8:28.
10. Proverbs 3:5–6.
11. Luke 10:20.

Chapter Ten, Rebuilding
1. Romans 13:14.
2. Daniel 1:8.
3. 1 Corinthians 6:12; 8:13; 10:31.
4. Fred Smith, *Discipleship Journal,* Winter 1995, 38.
5. Matthew 28:18–20.
6. James 1:22.
7. 2 Timothy 3:16–17.
8. Matthew 6:5–15.
9. Matthew 7:7–11.
10. Matthew 6:33.
11. This substantive can also be translated the "evil thing" or "evil way."
12. Alfred Lord Tennyson, *Morte D'Arthur,* line 415.
13. John Newton, "Come, My Soul, Thy Spirit Prepare."
14. 1 Chronicles 4:9–10.

Chapter Eleven, Reconnecting
1. John Donne, "Meditation XVII."
2. Hebrews 10:25.
3. Ephesians 5:25.
4. Matthew 28:18–20.
5. Matthew 16:18.
6. John 4:23. Although this reference is a declaration that His people will worship the Lord in spirit and truth, it does not give reference to corporate worship. The practice of the early church, however, as well as the glimpses in Revelation point clearly to corporate worship.
7. John 13:34–35.
8. 2 Timothy 2:2.
9. Matthew 5:13–16.
10. Philippians 4:8–9.
11. Anonymous, *Inspiring Quotations,* 164.